D0938796

INTRODUCING
ISSUES WITH
OPPOSING
VIEWPOINTS®

Taxes and Society's Priorities

Caleb Bissinger, Book Editor

GREENHAVEN
PUBLISHING

Published in 2018 by Greenhaven Publishing, LLC
353 3rd Avenue, Suite 255, New York, NY 10010

Articles in Greenhaven Publishing anthologies are often edited for length to meet page requirements. In addition, original titles of these works are changed to clearly present the main thesis and to explicitly indicate the author's opinion. Every effort is made to ensure that Greenhaven Publishing accurately reflects the original intent of the authors. Every effort has been made to trace the owners of the copyrighted material.

Library of Congress Cataloging-in-Publication Data

Names: Bissinger, Caleb, editor.
Title: Taxes and society's priorities / Caleb Bissinger, book editor.
Description: First edition. | New York : Greenhaven Publishing, 2018. |
   Series: Introducing issues with opposing viewpoints | Includes
   bibliographical references and index. | Audience: Grades 9-12.
Identifiers: LCCN 2017042495| ISBN 9781534501928 (library bound) | ISBN
   9781534502765 (pbk.)
Subjects: LCSH: Taxation—United States—Juvenile literature. | Finance,
   Public—United States—Juvenile literature.
Classification: LCC HJ2381 .T3954 2018 | DDC 336.200973—dc23
LC record available at https://lccn.loc.gov/2017042495

Manufactured in the United States of America

Website: http://greenhavenpublishing.com

Contents

Foreword

Indulging in a wide spectrum of ideas, beliefs, and perspectives is a critical cornerstone of democracy. After all, it is often debates over differences of opinion, such as whether to legalize abortion, how to treat prisoners, or when to enact the death penalty, that shape our society and drive it forward. Such diversity of thought is frequently regarded as the hallmark of a healthy and civilized culture. As the Reverend Clifford Schutjer of the First Congregational Church in Mansfield, Ohio, declared in a 2001 sermon, "Surrounding oneself with only like-minded people, restricting what we listen to or read only to what we find agreeable is irresponsible. Refusing to entertain doubts once we make up our minds is a subtle but deadly form of arrogance." With this advice in mind, Introducing Issues with Opposing Viewpoints books aim to open readers' minds to the critically divergent views that comprise our world's most important debates.

Introducing Issues with Opposing Viewpoints simplifies for students the enormous and often overwhelming mass of material now available via print and electronic media. Collected in every volume is an array of opinions that captures the essence of a particular controversy or topic. Introducing Issues with Opposing Viewpoints books embody the spirit of nineteenth-century journalist Charles A. Dana's axiom: "Fight for your opinions, but do not believe that they contain the whole truth, or the only truth." Absorbing such contrasting opinions teaches students to analyze the strength of an argument and compare it to its opposition. From this process readers can inform and strengthen their own opinions or be exposed to new information that will change their minds. Introducing Issues with Opposing Viewpoints is a mosaic of different voices. The authors are statesmen, pundits, academics, journalists, corporations, and ordinary people who have felt compelled to share their experiences and ideas in a public forum. Their words have been collected from newspapers, journals, books, speeches, interviews, and the internet, the fastest growing body of opinionated material in the world.

Introducing Issues with Opposing Viewpoints shares many of the well-known features of its critically acclaimed parent series, Opposing

Viewpoints. The articles allow readers to absorb and compare divergent perspectives. Active reading questions preface each viewpoint, requiring the student to approach the material thoughtfully and carefully. Photographs, charts, and graphs supplement the articles. A thorough introduction provides readers with crucial background on an issue. An annotated bibliography points the reader toward articles, books, and websites that contain additional information on the topic. An appendix of organizations to contact contains a wide variety of charities, nonprofit organizations, political groups, and private enterprises that each hold a position on the issue at hand. Finally, a comprehensive index allows readers to locate content quickly and efficiently.

Introducing Issues with Opposing Viewpoints is also significantly different from Opposing Viewpoints. As the series title implies, its presentation will help introduce students to the concept of opposing viewpoints and learn to use this material to aid in critical writing and debate. The series' four-color, accessible format makes the books attractive and inviting to readers of all levels. In addition, each viewpoint has been carefully edited to maximize a reader's understanding of the content. Short but thorough viewpoints capture the essence of an argument. A substantial, thought-provoking essay question placed at the end of each viewpoint asks the student to further investigate the issues raised in the viewpoint, compare and contrast two authors' arguments, or consider how one might go about forming an opinion on the topic at hand. Each viewpoint contains sidebars that include at-a-glance information and handy statistics. A Facts About section located in the back of the book further supplies students with relevant facts and figures.

Following in the tradition of the Opposing Viewpoints series, Greenhaven Publishing continues to provide readers with invaluable exposure to the controversial issues that shape our world. As John Stuart Mill once wrote: "The only way in which a human being can make some approach to knowing the whole of a subject is by hearing what can be said about it by persons of every variety of opinion and studying all modes in which it can be looked at by every character of mind. No wise man ever acquired his wisdom in any mode but this." It is to this principle that Introducing Issues with Opposing Viewpoints books are dedicated.

Introduction

"To compel a man to furnish funds for the propagation of ideas he disbelieves and abhors is sinful and tyrannical."
— *Thomas Jefferson*

"Taxes, after all, are dues that we pay for the privileges of membership in an organized society."
—*Franklin D. Roosevelt*

I n this world nothing can be said to be certain," Benjamin Franklin quipped, "except death and taxes." We live. We die. We pay our dues. So it has always been. In ancient Mesopotamia, a society without currency, the government required all men to complete "burden"—months of hard labor digging canals, tilling fields, taking up arms. In 325 CE, Roman emperor Constantine the Great levied *collatio lustralis*, a tax on all trade to be paid in gold. In colonial America in July 1619, twenty-two men gathered in the Jamestown Church and established the colony's first tax. It required that every man over the age of sixteen harvest ten pounds of tobacco. The certainty of taxation had arrived in the New World, and it has stayed here ever since. In 1773, sixty men dumped 342 chests of English tea into Boston Harbor. The Boston Tea Party, we call it, a rebellion against a sneaky bit of tax manipulation from British Parliament, which assumed the power to levy whatever taxes it pleased on its colonies. Those sixty men—and many absent others—had had enough with England's tyrannical ways. No taxes without representation, they said, and into the drink went the tea.

What exactly is a tax? Merriam Webster defines it thus: "a charge usually of money imposed by authority on persons or property for public purposes." Taxes come in all shapes and sizes. We pay sales tax on the things we buy and sin tax on the things we shouldn't (cigarettes, alcohol, soda). We pay property tax on the homes we own. We pay estate tax on the money we inherit. And, of course, we pay income tax on the money we earn. Where does it all go? Well, our taxes pay for Social Security, Medicare and Medicaid, education, national defense, scientific research, arts funding, and many other things.

For almost a hundred years, there was no income tax in the United States, but during the Civil War, Congress ratified the Revenue Act of 1861 to generate revenue for wartime expenditures. It lasted a decade. In 1894, Congress passed another income tax, but the Supreme Court decided it was unconstitutional on the grounds that the Constitution does not give the government the power to levy a direct tax. Then there came the Sixteenth Amendment, which gave Congress the authority to levy a direct income tax. It started small at around 1 percent. From 1932 to 1945, a span that encompassed both the Great Depression and the Second World War, the top marginal tax rate, paid by the wealthiest Americans, went from 63 percent all the way to 94 percent.

There is a seductive economic theory, which you'll read about in the pages that follow, that says lower taxes empower the economy by leaving individuals and businesses with more money to spend, invest, and expand. Now, a great many economists will tell you that this theory doesn't hold water. Others argue that taxes, government spending, and economic productivity are caught in a complicated love triangle that a tax cut won't settle. From 1981 and 1986, President Ronald Reagan cut the nation's top tax rate by 42 percent. President George W. Bush initiated sweeping tax cuts with the goal of healing the economy. Alas, a decade later, the *Washington Post* found those cuts increased the deficit, drove up income inequality, and disproportionately benefited the wealthiest Americans. And yet, today, President Donald Trump has promised to deliver the largest tax cuts ever.

"Death, taxes and childbirth!" Margaret Mitchell wrote in *Gone with the Wind*. "There's never any convenient time for any of them." Suffice it to say, some folks are awash with despair and resentment while they write out their checks to the IRS. But as Vanessa Williamson, a fellow at Harvard, discovered when she conducted a major poll to sniff out Americans' attitudes toward taxes, most of us think of taxpaying as a civic duty and find it to be a wellspring of pride. As one philosopher put it, "Paying taxes is the single most generous act we perform in relation to our fellow human beings." Taxes have a moral dimension. They are our contribution to the shared project of society. Senator Elizabeth Warren described it thus: "There is nobody in this country who got rich on their own. Nobody. You built a factory out there—good for you. But I want to be clear. You moved your goods to market on roads the rest of us paid for. You hired workers the rest of us paid to educate. You were safe in your factory because of police forces and fire forces that the rest of us paid for. You didn't have to worry that marauding bands would come and seize everything at your factory… Now look. You built a factory and it turned into something terrific or a great idea—God bless! Keep a hunk of it. But part of the underlying social contract is you take a hunk of that and pay forward for the next kid who comes along."

In the viewpoints that follow, you will encounter a diverse range of opinions about taxation. Some authors will argue that taxation is nothing more than theft; others will argue that taxes are, on the contrary, essential for ensuring the nation's well being. You'll learn about the sometimes paternal relationship between the government and its taxpayers, the use of taxation to protect the environment, and the ways in which some economists believe we could successfully redesign our tax system. Undoubtedly, taxes built this society. What's left for exploration in *Introducing Issues with Opposing Viewpoints: Taxes and Society's Priorities* is to trace the historical, moral, and theoretical components of its legacy.

Chapter 1

Why Do We Pay Taxes?

Taxes are charged and collected to build a society.

Our Taxation System Has Only Caused Problems

"I believe God did give mankind unlimited gifts to invent, produce and create. And for that reason it would be wrong for governments to devise a tax structure that suppresses those gifts."

Bill Federer

In the following viewpoint, Bill Federer traces the history of the federal income tax from the Civil War, when it was first introduced, into modern times. Federer makes several striking—and disputable—claims. The perpetuation of the income tax, he argues, engendered massive government spending and debt, inspired political corruption, and inspired nonprofit entities that Federer dislikes. However, he chooses not to devote any space to the ostensible benefits of the income tax, such as education, national defense, and scientific research. Federer is the author of *Change to Chains: The 6,000 Year Quest for Global Control* and *What Every American Needs to Know About the Quran*.

AS YOU READ, CONSIDER THE FOLLOWING QUESTIONS:

1. Before the introduction of the direct federal income tax, where did the government's revenue come from?
2. How did John F. Kennedy and John Maynard Keynes view taxes differently?
3. Who founded the American Civil Liberties Union (ACLU)?

"How Our Taxation System Screwed Everything Up," by Bill Federer, WND.com, April 14, 2017. Reprinted by permission.

On April 15, 1865, President Lincoln died. He was shot the night before in Ford's Theater.

On April 15, 1912, the *Titanic* sank. It struck an iceberg the night before. Among the 1,514 lives lost were millionaires John Jacob Astor IV, Benjamin Guggenheim, and Isa Strauss, all of whom were vocal opponents of the Federal Reserve Act.

In 1954, April 15 became the deadline for filing income tax returns.

Originally, Article I, Section 9 of the US Constitution prohibited a direct federal income tax on American citizens: "No capitation or other direct tax shall be laid, unless in proportion to the census or enumeration hereinbefore directed to be taken."

The federal government's revenue was derived from excise taxes on specific items like salt, tea, tobacco, etc., and tariff taxes on imports. Prior to the Civil War, most tariff taxes were collected at Southern ports, like Charleston, South Carolina. Tariffs made foreign goods more expensive, motivating people to buy domestically produced goods, made mostly in Northern factories. The South had few factories, as its economy was based on agricultural crops, mostly cotton and rice, which unfortunately relied heavily on slave labor. Thus, the tariff taxes that helped the North, hurt the South.

During the Civil War, Republican President Abraham Lincoln passed an emergency "Revenue" income tax to help fund the Union. It was repealed in 1873.

The first non-emergency "peacetime" income tax was attempted in 1894, but the Supreme Court declared it unconstitutional in *Pollock v Farmers' Loan*.

Justice Stephen J. Field concurred: "The income tax law under consideration ... is class legislation. Whenever a distinction is made in the burdens a law imposes or in the benefits it confers on any citizens by reason of their birth, or wealth, or religion, it is class legislation, and leads inevitably to oppression and abuses. ..."

Justice Field continued: "It is the same in essential character as that of the English income statute of 1691, which taxed Protestants at a certain rate, Catholics, as a class, at double the rate of Protestants, and Jews at another and separate rate."

The delegates at the Constitutional Convention gave the federal government the power to levy taxes.

Industrialists helped bring about the greatest rise in the standard of living for the average person, with more goods at cheaper prices, than ever before in world history. Industrialists then began to create monopolies, influence political parties and plot to gain control of the banking system.

Republican President Theodore Roosevelt attempted to limit their power with an inheritance tax. Republican President William Taft yielded to mounting public pressure to tax these rich industrialists by placing a two percent tax on corporate profits, as only the wealthiest owned corporate stock.

With World War I threatening, Democrat President Woodrow Wilson naively thought that if tariff taxes between countries were eliminated there would be world peace. Wilson proposed replacing the lost tariff revenue with an income tax on the wealthy. This was passed in 1913 with the 16th Amendment.

Originally, the income tax was a one percent tax on the top one percent richest people. It was a type of "soak-the-rich" tax only intended for industrialists such as Rockefeller, Carnegie, Vanderbilt, Fisk, Flagler, Gould, Harriman, Mellon, J.P. Morgan and Schwab.

Industrialists strategically avoided paying the income tax by transferring their assets into tax-exempt charitable and educational foundations, such as the Rockefeller Foundation and Carnegie Foundation.

This tax-exempt category had previously been for churches, which historically were the providers of social welfare through their hospitals, medical clinics, orphanages, schools and soup kitchens, where they cared for orphans, widows, maimed soldiers, prisoners, unwed mothers, widows, shut-ins, homeless, juvenile delinquents and immigrants.

Churches also provided a significant social service by instilling morals and virtues into the nation's population. This helped reduce crime, child abuse, broken homes, derelicts, and other social ills, which, since the relinquishing of these responsibilities to government, have become an immense financial burden on taxpayers, being, in many cases, the largest items on State budgets.

In 1942, with World War II, Democrat President Franklin Roosevelt increased and expanded the federal income tax with "the greatest tax bill in American history," even instituting paycheck withholding.

John F. Kennedy stated April 20, 1961: "In meeting the demands of war finance, the individual income tax moved from a selective tax imposed on the wealthy to the means by which the great majority of our citizens participate in paying."

Beardsley Ruml, chairman of Macy's Department Store, became director of the New York Federal Reserve Bank, where he promoted the idea of withholding taxes from people's paychecks.

Kennedy explained, April 20, 1961: "Withholding … on wages and salaries (was) … introduced during the war when the income tax was extended to millions of new taxpayers."

Businesses gradually became subject to:

- Higher taxes
- Higher wages and benefits
- More lawsuits
- More governmental bureaucracy
- More environmental restrictions
- Political favoritism, or "cronyism," toward some companies at the expense of others

Businesses that did not receive this favoritism began to be faced with the alternative of going out of the country or going out of business. As companies outsourced jobs to stay competitive in the growing global market, patriotic attachments diminished, giving rise to financial globalists.

John F. Kennedy noticed, February 6, 1961: "I have asked the secretary of the treasury to report on whether present tax laws may be stimulating in undue amounts the flow of American capital to the industrial countries abroad."

Kennedy told Congress, April 20, 1961: "In those countries where income taxes are lower than in the United States, the ability to defer the payment of US tax by retaining income in the subsidiary companies provides a tax advantage for companies operating through overseas subsidiaries that is not available to companies operating solely in the United States."

To remedy this, Democrat President John F. Kennedy proposed a stimulus plan of lowering taxes across-the-board, as he stated Sept. 18, 1963: "A tax cut means higher family income and higher business profits and a balanced Federal budget. Every taxpayer and his family will have more money left over after taxes for a new car, a new home, new conveniences, education, and investment. Every businessman can keep a higher percentage of his profits in his cash register or put it to work expanding or improving his business, and as the national income grows, the federal government will ultimately end up with more revenues."

Kennedy stated Jan. 17, 1963: "Lower rates of taxation will stimulate economic activity and so raise the levels of personal and corporate income as to yield within a few years an increased—not a reduced—flow of revenues to the federal government."

Kennedy stated, Nov. 20, 1962: "It is a paradoxical truth that tax rates are too high and tax revenues are too low and the soundest way to raise the revenues in the long run is to cut the rates now. ... Cutting taxes now is not to incur a budget deficit, but to achieve the more prosperous, expanding economy which can bring a budget surplus."

John F. Kennedy stated in his annual message, Jan. 21, 1963: "In today's economy, fiscal prudence and responsibility call for tax reduction even if it temporarily enlarges the federal deficit—why reducing taxes is the best way open to us to increase revenues. ... It is no contradiction—the most important single thing we can do to stimulate investment in today's economy is to raise consumption by major reduction of individual income tax rates."

JFK mentioned in his message to Congress on tax reduction, Jan. 24, 1963: "Our tax system still siphons out of the private economy too large a share of personal and business purchasing power and reduces the incentive for risk, investment and effort—thereby aborting our recoveries and stifling our national growth rate."

Whereas Kennedy wanted to reduce taxes to stimulate the economy, economist John Maynard Keynes had proposed stimulating the economy by going in debt. John Maynard Keynes reasoned that if the government went in debt spending money in the private sector to create jobs, those jobs would pay taxes and pay off the debt.

Unfortunately, politicians were tempted to continually increase debt in order to funnel money to their districts and constituencies to help them get reelected, hoping the next Congress would be responsible and pay it off. The Keynesian debt-stimulated economy has resulted in an unsustainable $19 trillion US national debt.

On the other side of the world, Vladimir Lenin's plan to institute socialism included eliminating business owners, called "bourgeoisie": "The way to crush the bourgeoisie is to grind them between the millstones of taxation and inflation." Lenin stated: "The goal of socialism is communism."

Regarding socialism, President Ford later stated in Rock Hill, South Carolina, Oct. 19, 1974: "What they don't tell us when they propose all these benefits that they are going to give you from our

Government … that a government big enough to give us everything we want is a government big enough to take from us everything we have."

After the 1917 Bolshevik Revolution in Russia, Communist labor organizers, community organizers, agitators, and agent provocateurs (provoking agents) infiltrated other countries, including the United States. They utilized the tactic of psychological projection or "blame-shifting" where the attacker blames the victim.

Sigmund Freud wrote in "Case Histories II" (PFL 9, p. 132) of "psychological projection" where humans resort to the defensive mechanism of denying in themselves the existence of unpleasant behavior while attributing that exact behavior to others. A rude person constantly accuses others of being rude.

Marx is attributed with the phrase "Accuse the victim of what you do" or "Accuse your opponent of what you are guilty of":

- If you are lying, accuse your opponent of it.
- If you are racist, accuse your opponent of it.
- If you are sexually immoral, accuse your opponent of it.
- If you are engaging in voter fraud, accuse your opponent of it.
- If you are disseminating "fake news," accuse your opponent of spreading it.
- If you are receiving millions from globalist and Hollywood elites, accuse your opponent of being controlled by the rich.

Political advisor David Axelrod verbalized this Machiavellian tactic in an NPR interview, April 19, 2010: "In Chicago, there was an old tradition of throwing a brick through your own campaign office window, and then calling a press conference to say that you've been attacked."

Agitating groups formed tax-exempt educational foundations to fundamentally change the government by instigating a workers' revolution. Naive individuals recruited to join their ranks were referred to by Lenin as "useful idiots."

In 1917, Roger Baldwin founded a tax-exempt organization to defend those who opposed World War I and were accused of being Communist agitators. It was renamed the ACLU.

In 1921, Margaret Sanger founded the tax-exempt organization to eliminate "human weeds" and promote racial "purification." It was renamed Planned Parenthood.

The growth of tax-exempt organizations advocating change resulted in the Congress attempting to limit what tax-exempt organizations could do politically.

Commenting on the increased size of government and tax burden, President Ronald Reagan remarked at the National Space Club Luncheon, March 29, 1985: "Personally, I like space. The higher you go, the smaller the federal government looks."

Reagan stated in 1988: "I believe God did give mankind unlimited gifts to invent, produce and create. And for that reason it would be wrong for governments to devise a tax structure that suppresses those gifts."

EVALUATING THE AUTHOR'S ARGUMENTS:

Viewpoint author Federer believes taxation inspired the formation of socially minded nonprofit organizations. While he is disparaging of these organizations, can you think of ways in which nonprofits, such as the American Red Cross, the ASPCA, and the Mayo Clinic, have been good for society?

Income Taxes Foster Economic Justice

Erik Loomis

"The income tax was the most popular economic justice movement of the late 19th and early 20th century."

In the following viewpoint, Erik Loomis provides a progressive argument for the income tax. Looking to history, he points out that the income tax was initially popular with the citizenry because it replaced indirect taxes on popular items like alcohol and tobacco, and because it leveled the playing field. In the last half-century, the middle class has grown (and those individuals have seen their tax burdens grow, too), and few hold taxes in high regard. But Loomis argues that an aggressive tax increase on the wealthiest Americans would mark a major step toward restoring economic justice. Loomis is a professor at the University of Rhode Island.

AS YOU READ, CONSIDER THE FOLLOWING QUESTIONS:
1. According to the author, what was "the most popular economic justice movement of the late 19th and early 20th century"?
2. What is an *indirect tax*?
3. For what three reasons does the author believe the income tax has grown unpopular in the last half-century?

"The Hidden Progressive History of Income Tax," by Erik Loomis, AlterNet, September 7, 2012. Reprinted by permission.

Imagine a United States with enormous and growing levels of income inequality. An America with long-term unemployment and people giving up hope for the future. An America where corporations buy politicians and ignore the desires of everyday people. An America where a lack of regulation leads to a boom-and-bust economy that allows the 1% to get even more wealthy while throwing millions of Americans out of work.

That I could be talking about today or the Gilded Age is telling. The end of the 19th century saw corporations at their height of influence and power, with plutocrats literally buying off legislatures to elect their men to the US Senate and individuals like John D. Rockefeller and J.P. Morgan having more money than the entire federal government.

Americans fixed a lot of these problems in the 20th century. The mid-20th century was a period when more Americans had a larger share of the pie, with a growing middle-class, high rates of unionization, an expanding consumer economy leading to home ownership, working-class people going to college without much debt, and a better life for all, even if too often minorities were denied inclusion in this society.

We have to understand the ways our ancestors fought to even the playing field. How did they take power from the rich in the early 20th century, a time when the plutocrats had even more power than the present? After much debate, they settled on a solution that went a long way toward making the United States a more fair country.

Income Taxes

Today, we are supposed to hate paying taxes. They are our "tax burden." We vote for politicians who will reduce our taxes, even if that means destroying the welfare state. Conservatives' century-long war against taxes has paid off by convincing everyday Americans to think taxes are a horrible thing that pays for government waste.

Our ancestors knew this was not true. The income tax was the most popular economic justice movement of the late 19th and early 20th century. This truly grassroots movement forced politicians to act in order to stay in office, leading to the 16th Amendment to the Constitution in 1913. That's right, the income tax was so popular

Sixty-first Congress of the United States of America;

At the First Session,

Begun and held at the City of Washington on Monday, the fifteenth day of March, one thousand nine hundred and nine.

JOINT RESOLUTION

Proposing an amendment to the Constitution of the United States.

Resolved by the Senate and House of Representatives of the United States of America in Congress assembled (two-thirds of each House concurring therein), That the following article is proposed as an amendment to the Constitution of the United States, which, when ratified by the legislatures of three-fourths of the several States, shall be valid to all intents and purposes as a part of the Constitution:

"ARTICLE XVI. The Congress shall have power to lay and collect taxes on incomes, from whatever source derived, without apportionment among the several States, and without regard to any census or enumeration."

Speaker of the House of Representatives.

Vice-President of the United States and
President of the Senate.

Attest:

The Sixteenth Amendment to the US Constitution allows the federal government to collect a tax on income, independent of state collections.

that the nation passed a constitutional amendment so that the right-wing Supreme Court couldn't overturn it.

Income and Tax Inequality in the Late 19th Century

Everyday Americans hated the tax system of the Gilded Age. The federal government gathered taxes in two ways. First, it placed high tariff rates on imports. These import taxes protected American industries from competition. This allowed companies to charge high prices on products that the working class needed to survive while also protecting the monopolies that controlled their everyday lives. Second, the government had high excise taxes on tobacco and alcohol, two products used heavily by the American working class.

These forms of indirect taxes meant that almost the entirety of federal tax revenue came from the poor while the rich paid virtually nothing. This spawned enormous outrage. The poor had a model in creating an income tax—President Abraham Lincoln, who instituted the nation's first income tax to pay for the Civil War. Lincoln's Revenue Act of 1861 created a graduated tax on everyone who made at least $800 a year, allowing him to pay for the war. Although a grand success, Republicans pulled away from it as they backed off of racial equality in the late 1860s and it was overturned in 1872.

At first, Americans did not protest much against the end of the income tax, but with skyrocketing income inequality of the Gilded Age, grassroots movements sprung up to find solutions. Many Americans were attracted to simple one-size-fits-all ideas like Henry George's Single Tax, intended to pay for all government expenditures by taxes on land transactions that supporters also hoped would draw urban dwellers back to the farms.

Others supported taxing the rich directly. As historian Ajay K. Mehrotra has shown, grassroots organizations across the country began organizing around replacing the tariff with the income tax. He tells the story of Merlinda Sisins of Pickleville, Michigan, a mother of 16 who, despite a lack of education and poor spelling, began writing letters to the *Journal of United Labor*, where she demanded that working people nominate their own to Congress in order to pass legislation that would destroy the tariff and the monopolies.

Not all working-class people jumped on board with the income tax immediately. Some worried it would give the government too much power. Many labor unions worried that lowering the tariff could cost them their jobs. The Knights of Labor, the nation's most important labor union in the 1880s, tried to avoid the question because members in protected industries supported the tariff while other workers knew it made them poorer.

The Panic of 1893 and the Rise of the Graduated Income Tax

This all changed with the Panic of 1893. The nation's greatest economic collapse before the Great Depression, the Panic started with a popped railroad bubble, leading to bank collapses. Nearly 20% of workers were unemployed by 1894. Outrage over the way greedy monopolists had sabotaged the economy and the government's feeble response propelled the income tax to the center of American reform.

This dovetailed with the rise of the People's Party, or Populists. These farmers, mostly located on the Great Plains and in the South, organized themselves during the 1880s and 1890s to take back control of the nation from corrupt urban monopolists. Their demands included government regulation of railroads and inflationary monetary policy that would help them pay their debts. They also supported the graduated income tax so the rich would finally pay their fair share. Their rise in the 1890s threatened the corrupt political consensus that gripped both parties during the Gilded Age. Organized labor now got on board with the income tax as well, as the turmoil of the Panic of 1893 convinced even many workers in tariff-protected industries of the need for the income tax.

The income tax became such an overwhelming political move-ment during the 1890s that Congress, despite so many members' close relationship with the plutocracy, passed an income tax law that would have forced the rich to begin paying income taxes for the first time since 1870. The Wilson-Gorman Tariff of 1894 placed a 2% tax on incomes over $4000 a year (approximately $88,000 today).

Corporations immediately organized against this. In a strategy we can recognize today, the Chamber of Commerce distorted the bill's purpose, telling the public that the income tax would drive them into poverty, even though the bill did not affect working-class people. Yet the Chamber made little headway in the face of this overwhelmingly popular movement.

But the Supreme Court in 1895 declared the federal income tax unconstitutional in the case of *Pollock v. Farmers' Loan & Trust Company*. This was the same set of judges who ruled segregation consti-tutional in the case of *Plessy v. Ferguson* and followed that up with a number of court cases that both concentrated wealth in the hands of the few and oppressed minority populations, including Mexican Americans in New Mexico and Native Americans.

Yet the income tax movement continued, now with the goal of a constitutional amendment to overcome a hostile Court. Over the next 15 years, a variety of reform movements, including farmers, organized labor, and, increasingly, middle-class reformers known as Progressives, pushed for the income tax to alleviate America's stubborn inequality and to provide the government more money in order to function as modern 20th-century state. Despite continued corporate opposition, Congress presented a constitutional amendment to the states in 1909, which finally achieved ratification in 1913 as the 16th Amendment. Over the next century, income taxes played an enormous role in level-ing the national playing field and creating the middle class.

Lessons for Today

So how did we become a nation where the working and middle classes have turned on progressive taxation? I argue for three major reasons. First, the great success of the 20th century state to create a middle class then allowed conservatives to claim that they represented everyday taxpayers, a claim the new middle class found all too believable once they started paying higher taxes.

Second, the growth of the social safety net combined with white backlash to the civil rights movement in the 1960s and 1970s to create a racial code around taxes that suggested white taxpayers subsidized, for instance, black mothers on welfare.

Third, the ability of the extreme rich like Mitt Romney to avoid paying taxes through creating loopholes and offshore accounts has created resentment toward the entire system: if Romney isn't paying taxes, why should I?

Progressives need to reclaim income tax rates as an organizing issue. We need to press for an aggressive tax increase on the wealthy while lowering income taxes for those who can't afford to pay them. We should also call for vigorous prosecution of tax cheats, the closing of tax loopholes, and a series of government programs directly paid for by the income taxes from the wealthy. This is a tall order in the face of the current anti-tax mentality. But until we reclaim the mantle of progressive taxation, we won't have access to a primary tool to create a more just and equitable society.

EVALUATING THE AUTHOR'S ARGUMENTS:

Viewpoint author Loomis argues that middle class expansion, racial mistrust, and the exploitation of tax loopholes by the very rich have all contributed to the national dislike of taxes. How, then, can progressives reassure people that the income tax is, in fact, a tool for securing economic justice?

FDR's New Deal Proves the Value of Fiscal Expansion

Marshall Auerback

"[One] lesson of the Great Depression is that properly targeted fiscal policy which focuses on job creation can work."

When conservative economists try to illustrate that when taxes are raised the economy suffers, they point to 1937, the year the United States' recovery from the Great Depression sputtered. In the following viewpoint, Marshall Auerback rebukes that theory. While he concedes that tax increases can undercut private-sector activity, he argues that what was true in 1937 is still true today: The shift from fiscal expansion to austerity is a good way to hobble the economy. Auerback argues that the best lesson from the post-Depression recovery is that higher taxes, federal spending, and work programs bring down unemployment and bring up wages. Only when President Roosevelt turned against this strategy, opting instead to focus on deficit reduction, did the recovery falter. Auerback is a senior fellow at the Roosevelt Institute.

"The Real Lesson from the Great Depression: Fiscal Policy Works!" by Roosevelt Institute, Roosevelt Institute, August 30, 2010. Reprinted by permission.

AS YOU READ, CONSIDER THE FOLLOWING QUESTIONS:
1. Does the author believe that unions have any power in the United States today?
2. What did FDR's workfare program accomplish, according to the author?
3. How did FDR's fiscal policy change in his second term, as explained in the viewpoint?

I f the US government had a dollar every time someone proclaimed to learn the lessons of the Great Depression, we probably wouldn't have a budget deficit. Usually, these debates turn on the question of fiscal policy and whether in fact, FDR's New Deal had a discernable role in generating recovery. "Fiscal austerians" have done much to dismiss the economic achievements of the New Deal, some even suggesting that FDR's fiscal policies worsened the crisis.

For a brief period during 2008, the views of neo-liberals like Alan Greenspan and Robert Rubin were shunted aside. But the FDR revisionists, who disapprove of fiscal policy measures of any kind, have come back. Now they're brandishing the old arguments that "excessive" government spending risks "crowding out" private spending, making it impossible for the US government to deal with the recession (because it has run out of money) and hindering the capacity of the private sector to recover because of too much government interference in the "free market." These complaints are usually accompanied by a wave of rhetoric condemning the "business un-friendly" policies of the current Administration, along with dire warnings of a "national solvency" crisis. After all, fiscal austerians are nothing, if not fully predictable.

Was the 1937 Relapse Caused by Increased Taxes and Unions?

In that context, we have to give some credit to Professors Thomas Cooley and Lee Ohanian, who have taken a more novel approach in their critique of the New Deal. In some respects, they actually validate the case for fiscal policy expansion (although the two authors might not see it that way). Cooley and Ohanian argue that:

During the Great Depression, unemployment spiked and many hungry people were forced to rely on soup kitchens to provide daily sustenance.

> *The economy did not tank in 1937 because government spending declined. Increases in tax rates, particularly capital income tax rates, and the expansion of unions, were most likely responsible. Unfortunately, these same factors pose a similar threat today.*

The OMB numbers suggest that spending actually *did* decline in 1937 and 1938 and, contrary to the assertions of Cooley and Ohanian, that decline had a very deleterious impact on economic activity and employment. I will address the tax issue presently, but let's first deal with the "excessive unionization" canard. An objective observer looking at the US in the 21st century would hardly conclude that unions have any real power in the American economy today, any more that we have a "socialist" government dedicated to the promotion of a vast left wing agenda which enhanced union power. Obama has not addressed Labor Law reform and wages haven't risen in a generation; in fact, last year they fell.

True, the President occasionally does display a social democratic rhetoric, but so far, redistributive policies have primarily benefited financial institutions. Social security benefits are under threat via a new "bipartisan commission" on long term deficits, public health care insurance proposals were eviscerated in the "health care reform" bill, and trade unions outside the public sector have withered over the past 30 years. Cost of living adjustment clauses have largely disappeared since the early '80s (although some government benefits like social security retain them), average hourly earnings are virtually flat, and I would not be surprised to see wage deflation before the unemployment rate peaks this time around. US households are paying down debt on a net basis—even credit card debt—and creditors remain reluctant to make new loans. So the odds of a wage/price spiral taking root as a consequence of excessive union power look decidedly low—in fact, close to zero.

On the other question of taxes, I actually have some degree of sympathy with the arguments of Cooley and Ohanian, but largely because functionally, a tax increase works as a countercyclical policy which mitigates the impact of fiscal policy expansion.

Let's go back to basics. Under a fiat currency regime, such as we have in the US, when the Federal government spends, it electronically credits banks accounts. Taxation works exactly in reverse. Private bank accounts are debited (and private reserves fall) and the government accounts are credited and their reserves rise. All this is accomplished by accounting entries only, but the main point is that spending creates new net financial assets and taxation drains them.

So in one sense, Cooley and Ohanian are right. Tax hikes do cut aggregate demand, much as government spending cuts do. In economic terms, both serve to depress economic activity. We agree with the authors: tax rises at this juncture are a dumb idea. They won't serve to "reduce" the deficit, because the resultant impact on private sector activity is likely to diminish it and thereby increase the gap between government expenditures and revenues as the economy slows down.

The broader issue of government spending versus tax cuts is a political/distributional argument, and economists (and others) can legitimately argue about the respective multiplier effects of one versus the other. But at least this kind of discussion shifts the debate in the right direction—toward increasing economic activity and, hence, job growth and away from wrong-headed discussions of fiscal austerity and deficit reduction as a primary policy goal of government. FDR ran into trouble only when he moved away from fiscal expansion toward austerity in 1937.

At the outset of the Great Depression, economic output collapsed, and unemployment rose to 25 per cent. Influenced by his "liquidationist" Treasury Secretary, Andrew Mellon, then President Hoover made comparatively minimal attempts to deploy government fiscal policy to stimulate aggregate demand. Further, the Federal Reserve actually sold bonds to push up interest rates in a mindless effort to stem the gold outflows that we occurring as the rest of the world lost confidence in the US economy. So much for the halcyon days of the gold standard!

FDR's Employment and Wage Strategy Worked

This all changed under FDR. The key to evaluating Roosevelt's performance in combating the Depression is the statistical treatment of many millions of unemployed engaged in his massive workfare programs. The government hired about 60 per cent of the unemployed in public works and conservation projects that planted a billion trees, saved the whooping crane, modernized rural America, and built such diverse projects as the Cathedral of Learning in Pittsburgh, the Montana state capitol, much of the Chicago lakefront, New York's Lincoln Tunnel and Triborough Bridge complex, the Tennessee Valley Authority and the aircraft carriers *Enterprise* and *Yorktown.*

It also built or renovated 2,500 hospitals, 45,000 schools, 13,000 parks and playgrounds, 7,800 bridges, 700,000 miles of roads, and a thousand airfields. And it employed 50,000 teachers, rebuilt the country's entire rural school system, and hired 3,000 writers, musicians, sculptors and painters, including Willem de Kooning and Jackson Pollock. So much for the notion that government jobs are not "real jobs," as we hear persistently from critics of the New Deal!

The reasons for the discrepancies in the unemployment data that have historically arisen out of the New Deal are that the current sampling method of estimation for unemployment by the BLS was not developed until 1940. If these workfare Americans are considered to be unemployed, the Roosevelt administration reduced unemployment from 25 per cent in 1933 to 9.6% per cent in 1936, up to 13 per cent in 1938 (due largely to a reversal of the fiscal activism which had characterized FDR's first term in office), back to less than 1 per cent by the time the U.S. was plunged into the Second World War at the end of 1941.

In fact, once the Great Depression hit bottom in early 1933, the US economy embarked on four years of expansion that constituted the biggest cyclical boom in U.S. economic history. For four years, real GDP grew at a 12% rate and nominal GDP grew at a 14% rate. There was another shorter and shallower depression in 1937 largely caused by renewed fiscal tightening (and higher Federal Reserve margin requirements).

This economic relapse has led to the misconception that the central bank was pushing on a string throughout all of the 1930s, until the giant fiscal stimulus of the wartime effort finally brought the economy out of depression. That's factually incorrect. Most accounts of the Great Depression understate the effect of the New Deal job creation measures, because they don't show how much of the decline in official employment was attributable to the multiplier effect of spending on direct job creation. Also, the "work relief" category does not include employment on public works funded by the Public

Works Administration (PWA) nor the multiplier effect of PWA spending. The figures tell the story indirectly, however, in the path official unemployment followed—steeply declining in periods when work relief spending was high and either declining more slowly or increasing in periods when work relief spending was cut back. In fact, by the end of 1934, more than 20 million Americans (one out of six!) were receiving jobs or public assistance of one form or another from the "Welfare State."

Yes, 9.6% unemployment at the end of 1936 was still a big number. But it's hard to imagine the Democrats being in political peril for the midterms, or witnessing the current abysmal state of Obama's popularity ratings, if today's Administration could reduce unemployment by two-thirds in one term in office, as FDR did under any honest measure of unemployment. Suffice to say, unemployment reduction was the singular focus of the Roosevelt Administration; by contrast, today we have "the new normal," in effect, a faux intellectual argument to justify why we can't generate higher job growth. It's a testament to political failure.

In reference to the criticism of FDR's "high wage" policy by Cooley and Ohanian, it is worth noting that the wage "inflation" which they decry was in reality a product of a deflationary environment in which the general price level fell faster than the money wage level. During the outset of the Great Depression, output generation collapsed in the face of the US federal government's fiscal inaction and central bank interest rate hikes. This had the strange result of generating a counter-cyclical real wage increase, which in fact was nothing more than a product of depressed nature of the economy, in which overall prices were deflating prices faster than wages.

Overlaying the wage data with the true reduction in unemployment between 1933 to the end of 1936, makes it difficult to mount an empirical case that FDR wage improvements during the Great Depression were damaging to overall economic growth and increasing employment. Even if some sectors were disadvantaged (and that isn't proven by Cooley and Ohanian) the evidence actually suggests that the rises in real wages were associated with rising overall employment.

Relapse Caused by Austerity Measures

What about the relapse in 1937/38? By 1936 many economists and financial experts (notably FDR's Treasury Secretary, Henry Morgenthau) feared the country would go bankrupt if the government kept deficit-spending (sound familiar?). And after all, they argued, the government deficits had "pump-primed" the economy. The private sector could now take off on its own and get back to close to the full employment level of 1928–early 1929.

Consequently, Roosevelt ran (in 1936) on a platform that he would try to reduce, if not eliminate, the deficit. He won the election by a landslide—understandably, as the U.S. was out of depression by 1937. True to his campaign promise, government spending was cut significantly in 1937 and 1938, and taxes were raised to "fund" the new Social Security program. By 1938 Roosevelt submitted a budget in which the deficit was virtually eliminated (0.1% of GDP). The resultant economic relapse, based on efforts to balance the budget, exacerbated by a nonsensically tight monetary policy brought on by the Fed, duly followed.

This is unsurprising. Any type of fiscal austerity during a period of economic slowdown, whether via government spending cuts or higher taxes, will indeed depress economic activity.

But the other lesson of the Great Depression is that properly targeted fiscal policy which focuses on job creation can work. The Great Depression was indeed a disastrous human calamity but FDR's New Deal (including the high wage policies) attenuated the disaster. There is nothing to the claims that the interventions made things worse, other than when Roosevelt himself capitulated to the tired old forces of financial conservatism and fiscal austerianism, and the economy paid the price. Thankfully, FDR was not ideologically wed to the ideas of fiscal austerity and quickly reversed course. It helped, of course, that his Cabinet was well represented by progressive figures such as Frances Perkins, Henry Wallace, Harold Ickes and Harry Hopkins, who overcame the forces of economic conservatism embodied by FDR's Treasury Secretary, Henry Morgenthau. We need these kinds of progressive forces in current Administration, especially given the recent resignation of CEA head Christina Romer. It's time to let go of the old ideology, which created today's crisis. Here's hoping that President Obama, like FDR before him, changes course quickly. America is ready for a new New Deal.

EVALUATING THE AUTHOR'S ARGUMENTS:

Viewpoint author Auerback provides ample evidence that President Roosevelt's New Deal helped reduce unemployment from 25% to 9.6% in just three years. Do you agree with the author's claim that the policies put into place by the Roosevelt administration would be similarly effective today?

Taxes Are Beneficial to Both Our Economy and Our Society

"As our society has grown more complex, the increasing size of taxes we are willing to pay reflects the greater benefits we gain from the activities of government required to support it."

Matthew C. Weinzierl

The United States has what's called a progressive tax code. That means, simply, that the more you make, the higher your taxes are. The wealthiest among us have benefited greatly from our socety, and so it seems only fair that they contribute more than those who are less fortunate. This is the argument made by Matthew C. Weinzierl in the following viewpoint. But this fairness, Weinzierl asserts, is not without costs. It has undermined the poor, drying up cash assistance. And, on the other end of the spectrum, some wealthier Americans complain that their tax bills are far more than a fair share. Weinzierl is a professor at Harvard Business School.

"Why Americans Have Chosen to Pay Income Tax," by Matthew C. Weinzierl, the Conversation, April 13, 2015. https://theconversation.com/why-americans-have-chosen-to-pay-income-tax-39747. Licensed Under CC BY ND 4.0 International.

AS YOU READ, CONSIDER THE FOLLOWING QUESTIONS:
1. How did FDR define the Tax Law of 1913?
2. What did Oliver Wendell Holmes mean when he said, "I like to pay taxes. With them I buy civilization"?
3. How does the author define Americans' competing ideas of "fairness"?

We can be forgiven, especially this time of year, for questioning a decision our predecessors made just over a century ago. In the 1910s, Americans decided to make personal and corporate income taxes a permanent feature of the US economy.

Why did they start us down this road? And given that the taxes they endorsed started out small in scope and size but have multiplied by a factor of eight as a share of our economy, have we gone off course?

After all, when an income tax was introduced in 1862 to fund the Civil War, it lasted just six years before being replaced by other taxes. It took another 50 years before the 16th Amendment, which allows Congress to levy a national income tax, was adopted in 1913.

The Justification for a National Income Tax

One of the clearest statements of why Americans in the early 20th Century were willing to tax their incomes came from President Franklin Delano Roosevelt in the 1930s:

> With the enactment of the Income Tax Law of 1913, the Federal Government began to apply effectively the widely accepted principle that taxes should be levied in proportion to ability to pay and in proportion to the benefits received. Income was wisely chosen as the measure of benefits and of ability to pay.

Here, FDR sounds very much like an economics professor. He identifies a principle, a "guide," for policy that relies on abstract concepts like "ability to pay" and "benefits received."

But FDR is also saying something quite simple: if people do well, it is only right that they should help to pay for the setup that made

President Franklin D. Roosevelt signed the Social Security Act on August 14, 1935. Social Security alleviated the fear of poverty in retirement.

their success possible. More to FDR's point, people who do better should pay for more of that setup.

FDR's reasoning is far from obsolete; our current President seems to agree with him. In 2011, Barack Obama explained why he supported higher taxes on higher incomes:

> *As a country that values fairness, wealthier individuals have traditionally borne a greater share of this [tax] burden than the middle class or those less fortunate... [This is] a basic reflection of our belief that those who've benefited most from our way of life can afford to give back a little bit more.*

Obama Echoes Roosevelt's Sentiments

Like FDR, Obama wants us to see taxes not as a burden to be lamented but as a fair payment for benefits received. And as our society has grown more complex, the increasing size of taxes we are willing to pay reflects the greater benefits we gain from the activities of government required to support it.

President Obama disagreed on many policies with Mitt Romney, his opponent in the 2012 presidential election, but on this logic for taxation they are not so far apart. Lost in the press coverage of the president's 2012 rebuttal to anti-government forces "You didn't build that" was Romney's reply:

> [The President] describes people who we care very deeply about, who make a difference in our lives: our school teachers, firefighters, people who build roads. We need those things... You really couldn't have a business if you didn't have those things. But, you know, we pay for those things...in fact, we pay for them and we benefit from them.

It turns out that Romney, like Obama and FDR, views taxes as our way of paying for what we want government to do for us. As US Supreme Court justice Oliver Wendell Holmes famously said: "I like to pay taxes. With them I buy civilization."

Part of the appeal of this logic for taxes is that it seems fair. Each person paying for what they get reminds us of a group of friends who split the bill at dinner according to what they ordered.

But perhaps fairness demands something in addition, namely that we help those who are less fortunate. Some people appear to benefit very little from our economic system, earning little income and having even less to spend. Is it fair to ask them to contribute to the pool of taxes nevertheless, or should we focus on providing them with the opportunity to share the benefits most of us enjoy?

FAST FACT

Poverty is still a tragic problem in the United States. As of 2015, there were 43.1 million people living in poverty, and 19.4 million in extreme poverty (earning less than $10,000 a year for a family of four).

As President Obama said in 2013:

> *And the result is an economy that's become profoundly unequal and families that are more insecure…The combined trends of increased inequality and decreasing mobility pose a fundamental threat to the American Dream, our way of life, and what we stand for around the globe.*

Paying "Our Fair Share"

Americans have long balanced competing notions of fairness when deciding on policy toward the poor. We want everyone to pitch in, to pay their "fair share," so we have moved away from making cash transfers to low-income households and have avoided proposals for a minimum guaranteed income.

At the same time, we want to support those in need, to give them a "fair shot," so we make use of policies such as the earned income tax credit, childcare subsidies, and Medicaid to help people work their way into the broad middle class.

The same balance is at play in how we design policy toward the rich. We ask the highest earners among us to pay a greater share of their income than the rest of us. But, despite the well-known fact that inequality in incomes is now at levels not seen since FDR's time, President Obama faced stiff opposition in Congress when he sought to raise the marginal tax rate (the share of the next dollar earned that is paid in taxes) at the top of the income ladder.

Speaker of the House John Boehner, for example, argued that those high earners already paid their fair share: "The top one percent of wage earners in the United States pay 40 percent of the income tax. The people [the president is] talking about taxing are the very people that we expect to reinvest in our economy and to create jobs."

With the Presidential election of 2016 around the corner and political polarization at peak levels, debates over the purpose and fairness of taxation are once again front-and-center in US politics. Sometimes it can seem that these debates go around in circles, with partisans from both extremes advocating reforms that even they don't imagine becoming reality.

But we should celebrate these debates, for they are how we work our way toward an economic policy that reflects Americans' nuanced, evolving sense of fairness. They are a part of what makes our economy, and our society, work. And that knowledge might even make writing that check on April 15th a bit less painful.

EVALUATING THE AUTHOR'S ARGUMENTS:

Extrapolating from viewpoint author Weinzierl's argument, how does the current "fair share" tax system increase inequality and decrease mobility?

Chapter 2

Is Taxation a Practical or Moral Imperative?

Taxation has both practical and moral implications.

We Need a Progressive Income Tax, Just Ask Adam Smith

John Hill

"Progressive taxation is fair because the wealthy benefit disproportionately from the government."

In the following viewpoint, John Hill looks to Adam Smith, the eighteenth-century economist, to help him see how taxes fit into the social contract. Smith favored progressive taxes, where higher earners pay higher taxes. This system is fair, Hill posits, because the wealthy have so much to gain from the government. For example, government-funded scientific research empowers private sector innovation. American diplomacy makes international trade possible. The public education system produces legions of skilled workers. When infrastructure crumbles, it's hard to bring goods to market. Feeble tax revenue clogs the justice system and patent office, and scientific research peters out. Hill is the author of *Adam Smith's Equality and the Pursuit of Happiness* (2016).

"Taxes, the Social Contract, and Adam Smith," by John Hill, Massachusetts Foundation for the Humanities, March 25, 2015. Reprinted by permission.

AS YOU READ, CONSIDER THE FOLLOWING QUESTIONS:
1. What are Adam Smith's four principles of taxation?
2. How can a bridge's collapse undermine a corporation's bottom line?
3. What, according to the author, do we need in order to "achieve a fair social contract"?

Some people may be surprised that many citizens share [writer] Hayley Wood's characterization of taxes as her favorite social contract [in a 2015 blog post]. Even though the anti-tax crowd in the United States gets a lot of media play, many Americans understand that a social contract contains both rights and responsibilities. The Massachusetts Constitution is no exception.

The Massachusetts Constitution clearly states the right to tax as Hayley Wood shows in her recent blog. That Constitution also states clearly the benefits citizens receive:

> *Article VII. Government is instituted for the common good; for the protection, safety, prosperity and happiness of the people....*
>
> *Article X. Each individual of the society has a right to be protected by it in the enjoyment of his life, liberty and property, according to standing laws. He is obliged, consequently, to contribute his share of the expense of this protection; ... .*

Note the reciprocal responsibility to share the cost.

"A Badge of Liberty"

Some people may also be surprised by the things Adam Smith, "the father of capitalism," wrote about taxes. He wrote that they are a badge of liberty (poll-taxes on slaves are an exception).

Smith's four principles of taxation clearly state that taxes are part of a social contract. His first principle, that taxes should be based on ability to pay and based on the revenue one receives under protection of the state, has progressive taxation implications that few people

Like pledging allegiance to the flag, paying taxes is part of the social contract.

associate with Smith. In addition, he clearly emphasized progressive taxes in his arguments for higher house-rent tax rates for the wealthy stating that it was not unreasonable that the rich contribute to public expense something more than in proportion to their income. He made the same point about tolls on roads and about luxuries like silver and gold (which he called "superfluities"). The other principles specify that taxes should not be arbitrary, should be convenient to pay, and should be as low as possible.

But was Smith being fair arguing for higher tax rates for the rich? Let's look at his first principal again: pay based on what you are able to pay and based on what you receive in government services. Progressive taxation is fair because the wealthy benefit disproportionately from the government. Here are a few such services.

- Administration of justice
- Education
- Statutes of incorporation
- Defense and police functions that protect people and businesses at home and abroad

- Consular services by the Department of State that support American businesses involved in international trade
- Money and banking
- Patent protection
- Massive land grants to early railroad builders
- Support for innovation, such as the role of the federal government in developing passenger jet airplanes
- Medical and scientific research support
- Tax benefits for 401(k) plans that go disproportionately to the wealthy
- Infrastructure

Most of these services benefit everyone but the wealthy benefit more.

We can also look at this from another angle. If we starve the beast by keeping taxes so low that government operates ineffectively, we also make it more difficult for businesses to operate efficiently. When bridges collapse, that affects the bottom line of corporations that need to move raw materials and finished products into or out of that area. When Boston's public transportation virtually collapsed because of record-setting winter snowfall, business suffered. Did the blizzards cost $1 billion? Or more? And how much of that cost was because of the terrible performance by public transportation? Government failure years ago to provide the MBTA with resources adequate to fulfill its role imposed significant costs on businesses this winter.

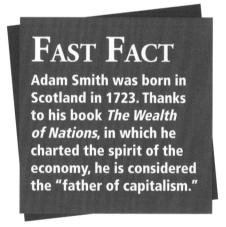

FAST FACT

Adam Smith was born in Scotland in 1723. Thanks to his book *The Wealth of Nations*, in which he charted the spirit of the economy, he is considered the "father of capitalism."

Regressive Taxes

In addition to his advocacy of progressive taxes, Smith opposed regressive taxation. He argued that taxes on necessities should be avoided because the poor find it difficult to get food, and so much of their income is spent on food.

The argument of this essay assumes that tax revenue is not wasted. It assumes that the government is a careful steward of both revenue and expenditures. It also assumes that, if we claim to be a capitalist market informed by the wisdom of the "father of capitalism," that we should heed his difficult lessons along with the more palatable ideas of the market economy. Ironically, if we were to accept the bitter with the sweet, our economy would be stronger and that would benefit everyone.

Do not tell me this essay advocates class warfare against the wealthy. Smith argued for fair treatment for all classes. This essay is also an argument for fairness. And it is an argument for a fair social contract not just for our generation, but for generations yet to be born. We have no right to impose immense government debts on future generations. To achieve a fair social contract, we need more government services; that will require higher taxes. We can do that and still be a capitalist society, consistent with the thought of Adam Smith.

EVALUATING THE AUTHOR'S ARGUMENTS:

Dr. Martin Luther King Jr. once said, "This country has socialism for the rich, rugged individualism for the poor." Public services, he felt, vastly favored corporations and the wealthy. Does the argument presented in John Hill's viewpoint support or undermine Dr. King's belief?

Sin Taxes Are Similar to Bad Parenting

"People are sometimes willing to accept excise taxes on such 'sinful' articles as tobacco and alcohol out of a feeling that these are a legitimate punishment."

James Sadowsky

In the following viewpoint, James Sadowsky takes issue with the implementation of sin taxes as a deterrent. It is perhaps only a slight exaggeration to say that the history of the world is the history of taxes. Loathing for taxes steeped the American Revolution. In France, *gabelle*, a tax on salt, so long aggrieved the citizenry that they rubbed it in the wound of the monarchy during their revolution. Both of those are examples of excise taxes—a tax levied on a particular commodity, like tea, salt, alcohol, or tobacco. But such taxes aren't merely a way to generate revenue. They also curtail the supply of certain goods but make said goods more expensive. Sadowsky was an emeritus professor of philosophy at Fordham University.

AS YOU READ, CONSIDER THE FOLLOWING QUESTIONS:
1. What is a sin tax?
2. What is the relationship between sin taxes, supply, and demand?
3. Why does the author accuse the government that levies sin taxes of being "paternalistic"?

"The Economics of Sin Taxes," by James Sadowsky, Acton Institute, July 20, 2010. Reprinted by permission.

Taxation on the purchase of nonessential and even harmful items, such as liquor and cigarettes, is known as a "sin tax."

S in Taxes" are so called because they are levied on those commodities, such as tobacco and alcohol, which are the objects of widespread disapproval. "Such taxes," Paul Samuelson says, "are often tolerated because most people—including many cigarette smokers and moderate drinkers—feel that there is something vaguely immoral about tobacco and alcohol. They think these 'sin taxes' stun two birds with one stone: the state gets revenue, and vice is made more expensive."

Excise Tax

"Sin Taxes" is not a technical term in economics. They are simply a form of excise tax. What, then, is an excise tax? It is a tax levied on *some* but not on *all* commodities. This is how it differs from the general sales tax, which is levied on all products (with certain minor exceptions). This means that it is levied in addition to the sales tax. Excise taxes have a long history. Remember the infamous salt tax under the French monarchy? There was the notorious tax on tea which was levied in the American colonies, which led to the Boston Tea Party and prepared the way for the American Revolution. Students of American history will recall the Whisky Insurrection, which occurred during the administration of George Washington. This rebellion grew out of resentment over an excise tax on whisky.

The long run effect of an excise tax is a reduction in the supply of the commodity on which the tax is levied. This in turn tends to lead to an increase in the price that consumers have to pay. How does this work itself out? If those who market the item continue to produce it in the same quantity, they will not be able to put up the price. If the consumers had been willing to pay the original price plus the tax, the producers could successfully have charged that amount in the absence of the tax. This would show that they had been charging less than the traffic would bear. And why not charge more for the product? After all, would they not have been taking advantage of any inelasticities of demand before the imposition of the tax?

So, if they continue to sell the same amount of the product on the market with the newly imposed tax, they will be unable to get any more than the old price. Since this price will not compensate them for the now higher costs of doing business, some firms will have to reduce the supply of the goods in question. The exiting of marginal firms from the industry as a result of the higher taxes contributes to the reduction of supply. This highlights the fact that producers do not directly control the prices at which their products will sell. Supply and demand determine the selling prices.

It is only by altering the supply or the demand that they are able to modify the price. And for all practical purposes we can rule out increasing demand as a means to offset higher production costs. Why? Because if manipulating demand was possible, they would have done so before the increase in production costs. So what changes the price is the diminution in the supply of the commodity. And, of course, this decrease in supply means that less of the article will be consumed.

Government Spending

What, then, are we to think of excise taxes? That depends, to no small degree, upon what we think of taxes in general. What is their purpose? Generally, it is to raise revenue for the government. In that case, we have to ask ourselves whether we want the government to have that revenue. The purpose of this revenue is to finance government spending. It is the spending rather than the removal of the money from our pockets that constitutes the main problem. Here is how Milton Friedman puts it in *Tyranny of the Status Quo*:

> However the government gets the money it spends, the goods and services that it buys, or that are bought by the people to whom it transfers money, are thereby not available for other use. Those goods and services—not the pieces of paper that pay for them—are the real cost of government to the taxpayers.

If the government were to take the money and toss it into the furnace, the main effect (supposing even-handed taxation) would be a decrease in the money supply. The remaining money would be sufficient to buy the same amount of goods and services because of the consequent reduction in prices. What matters, therefore, is the government's take in real terms: the goods and services that are no longer available and the consequent increase in prices. All the economist can do is to point out these costs. Whether they are worth bearing is a judgment call of another sort.

But here is a fact which escapes the notice of most people. It is not the case that the goods and services delivered by the government are in addition to the goods and services that were available before the government spending. They are instead of goods and services that would be otherwise available. Even people who do not pay taxes find themselves paying for these goodies in the form of higher prices for the things they really want. Politicians typically do not inform their constituencies of the cost that the benefits entail. When asked whether we want these things, we ought always to ask ourselves: "instead of what?" If people did this, they would be much less willing to endorse the current amount of government spending.

As we mentioned before, people are sometimes willing to accept excise taxes on such 'sinful' articles as tobacco and alcohol out of a feeling that these are a legitimate punishment for such indulgences. It is, therefore, not surprising that the government should eagerly tax these particular articles.

The Government as Parent

Sometimes, of course, the announced purpose of these taxes is to discourage the use of the product. They indeed do so if only because they decrease the quantity of the good. Many will wonder whether such paternalistic activity on the part of the government is warranted. They will ask themselves what makes politicians better judges of what is good for us than we ourselves or those persons in whose judgment we have confidence. Not only that—will the government stop there? Most likely not. The government is now threatening to move in on the use of vitamins and other nutritional items. We have come a long way from the days when it was accepted that the sole purpose of government was to protect the rights that were enumerated in the Declaration of Independence.

On occasion, "sin taxes" are defended because supposedly they both raise revenue and discourage the use of the sinful product. As John Bloom, the American Cancer Society's policy director said, "Canada has proven that tobacco taxes save lives and raise revenue." But one might ask whether a collision course is imminent here. Sin taxes do not raise revenue unless people use the product, and they do not save lives unless people avoid the product. Will not many of those who want to raise the revenue want people to commit the sin of using the product?

We can take comfort in the fact that a backlash seems to be finally taking place. According to the Feb. 9, 1994, *New York Times,* the Canadian Prime Minister, Jean Chretien, announced that Canada was slashing taxes on cigarettes to try to stamp out widespread smuggling from the United States, where taxes are currently about one-fifth as high. This shows that there are limits to what people in our day are willing to accept. Perhaps the great achievements of Thatcher-Reagan is not their legislative successes, but their shifting of the burden of proof from the private sector to the government.

EVALUATING THE AUTHOR'S ARGUMENTS:

The viewpoint author argues that when the government issues a sin tax in order to discourage its citizens from abusing that commodity, it has strayed from its duty. But doesn't the government also have a duty to safeguard the well being of its people? Is a tax on deleterious items, like tobacco, which is known to cause cancer, any different from the mandate that cars have seatbelts and roads speed limits?

A Sugar Tax Could Ultimately Help the Poor

Luke Allen

"Almost all consumption taxes are regressive; representing a proportionally higher share of low-income families' expendable income than those of the rich."

In the following viewpoint, Luke Allen explores the failed effort in the UK to implement a tax on sugary drinks. Advocates of the tax pointed out that, in addition to raising revenue, it would encourage people to turn to healthier drinks. But opponents noted that taxing sodas and other sugary drinks would disproportionately affect poor people. Allen argues that isn't such a bad thing, if it promotes good health. Some countries funnel such tax revenue toward programs and services for low-income families, he points out. Allen is a researcher at the University of Oxford.

AS YOU READ, CONSIDER THE FOLLOWING QUESTIONS:
1. How many people signed Jamie Oliver's tax petition?
2. What is "bandwidth tax"?
3. Why doesn't the author believe "soft measures" are effective?

When celebrity chef Jamie Oliver began campaigning for a tax on sugary drinks he expected a fight, and he was not disappointed.

"The food and drinks lobby might try to present me as a TV chef who has got too big for his boots," he wrote in the *Daily Mail*. "But I'm basing my arguments on the evidence of numerous doctors and scientists."

And Oliver certainly has the backing of healthcare professionals, not to mention the public.

Last month, amid much brouhaha, Public Health England (PHE) finally released its report recommending a tax on sugary soft drinks. The report had been commissioned by ministers to inform the government's upcoming child obesity strategy. Alison Tedstone, director of diet and obesity at PHE, had previously told MPs that a "fiscal approach" should be considered. The tax has broad based support from public health leaders, the British Medical Association (BMA), the World Health Organisation, global academics and the general public.

But in response to the 150,060 who signed a petition by Oliver in September 2015, the government announced it had "no plans to introduce a tax on sugar-sweetened beverages." Now David Cameron has personally vetoed the tax on the basis that it would disproportionately impact the poorest families. He seems to have misunderstood that this is a major strength of the policy.

Disincentive Is Stronger for the Poor

Almost all consumption taxes, including tobacco, alcohol and fuel, are regressive; representing a proportionally higher share of low-income families' expendable income than those of the rich. Health-related food taxes are no different and evidence demonstrates that the poor do indeed spend a proportionately higher amount on taxed unhealthy foods (although more revenue is generated from high-income households). This means that the financial disincentive is most potent for poorer families.

The poor are much more likely to have unhealthy diets and experience ill health than the rich. This leads to higher costs in the form of prescription co-payments, over the counter medications, travel to appointments and days off work for the self-employed. The inverse

Some politicians in the United States have suggested charging a sin tax for sugary sodas.

care law suggests those who need a health service most use it the least, and vice versa. As a result the poor are more likely to ignore existing health advice than the affluent who often already lead relatively healthy lives.

No Bandwidth Left

Behavioural economics and scarcity theory help to explain why poor people are less able to act in their own best interests. The main argument of the influential book *Scarcity: Why Having Too Little Means So Much* by Mullainathan and Shafir is that poverty imposes a mental processing "bandwidth tax" that focuses the mind on immediate concerns. For this reason educational campaigns and other "softer" interventions to help people eat more healthily can actually widen inequalities in health.

The rich and well-educated have the capacity to take on new information and change their behaviour to gain a future reward, such as getting a degree or losing weight. Poor people will find it much harder to give up immediate gratification for an uncertain, intangible future payoff. While it is possible to ignore "soft measures," such as educational campaigns and expanded healthcare services, increasing tax does not rely on the ability to make healthy choices. In fact, because the poor are more sensitive to changes in price, they respond better and experience larger health gains than the more affluent.

An OECD review of obesity prevention interventions concluded that taxes and other fiscal measures are the only interventions that consistently produce larger gains for the poor. This assertion was challenged by British researchers, but real-life evidence from Mexico showed the greatest gains for the poor. Compared with alternative measures such as education, tax has a much greater potential to improve the health of everyone while improving the health of the poor the fastest.

Part of the Solution

A sugary drinks tax is by no means a solution to the obesity crisis and would only ever constitute part of a broader strategy. Also the extent to which it falls on the poor depends on how the tax is devised and the different ways that rich and poor people respond to it. A tax on high-sugar organic yogurt will probably affect the rich more than a tax on cheap fizzy drinks. Similarly, if the poor are more likely to switch from buying taxed goods to relatively cheaper, and healthier, untaxed goods then they will bear less of the financial burden.

Evidence from research into taxes on sugar sweetened beverages shows that the amount of money spent each year on a sugary drinks tax is a tiny proportion of overall income; in the order of a few pounds. If the government is genuinely concerned about the fairness of this tax it can redress the balance through altering the rates of other taxes and benefits like tax credits and income tax thresholds. Some countries use the revenue generated by unhealthy food taxes to fund health services targeted at low-income families. It is the combination of all taxes and benefits that impacts the poor, not single policies in isolation.

To dismiss the policy out of hand because it has the greatest potential impact on those with the greatest burden of disease and the hardest behaviour to change is wrongheaded. Cameron should read the evidence laid out in the report commissioned by his government and re-examine his reasoning. If he really wants to help low-income families struggling to make healthier choices, surely the sugar tax is a perfect prescription.

EVALUATING THE AUTHOR'S ARGUMENTS:

Viewpoint author Luke Allen argues that the "rich and well-educated have the capacity to take on new information and change their behavior to gain a future reward" while "poor people are less able to act in their own best interests." Even if that is true, is it appropriate for the government to impose taxes meant to correct what it deems to be poor people's unhealthy, undesirable traits?

Politicians Oversimplify the Relationship Between Taxes and Economic Growth

"Candidates are presenting their dream worlds of fiscal policy, the way the US would operate if they could get everything they wanted through Congress."

Danielle Kurtzleben

In the following viewpoint, Danielle Kurtzleben fact checks the age-old argument that tax cuts foster economic growth and finds that the claim is dubious. Yes, targeted tax cuts can prove to be stimulating, but historically they have not been correlated to economic expansion. The author points to a survey in which zero percent of the economists polled agreed that cutting taxes would raise revenue in the next five years. The real takeaway, according to the author, is that politicians need to understand the complexity of the relationship between tax cuts and economic growth. Kurtzleben is a political reporter for NPR.

1. What percentage of economists, according to a University of Chicago survey, believe tax cuts boost the economy?
2. Why might tax cuts for lower income individuals lead to more economic growth than cuts for the wealthy?
3. What effect do economists believe tax cuts will have to short-term revenue?

I n Wednesday night's GOP debate, moderators pressed GOP candidates on their massive tax reform plans. Moderator John Harwood asked Donald Trump about the idea that his massive tax cuts would make the economy take off "like a rocket ship" (an idea that Trump staunchly defended).

Ted Cruz got at a similar idea, referencing the tax plan he unveiled Thursday: "[I]t costs, with dynamic scoring, less than $1 trillion. Those are the hard numbers. And every single income decile sees a double-digit increase in after-tax income. ... Growth is the answer. And as Reagan demonstrated, if we cut taxes, we can bring back growth."

The Big Question
Does reducing taxes grow the economy?

The Long Answer
Tax cuts can boost economic growth. But the operative word there is "can." It's by no means an automatic or perfect relationship.

We know, we know. No one likes a fact check with a nonfirm answer. So let's dig further into this idea.

There's a simple logic behind the idea that cutting taxes boosts growth: Cutting taxes gives people more money to spend as they like, which can boost economic growth.

Many—but by no means all—economists believe there's a relationship between cuts and growth. In a 2012 survey of top economists, the University of Chicago's Booth School of Business found that 35 percent thought cutting taxes would boost economic growth.

Some economists and politicians believe that tax cuts can lead to economic growth, including a booming urban expansion.

A roughly equal share, 35 percent, were uncertain. Only 8 percent disagreed or strongly disagreed.

But in practice, it's not always clear that tax cuts themselves automatically boost the economy, according to a recent study.

"[I]t is by no means obvious, on an ex ante basis, that tax rate cuts will ultimately lead to a larger economy," as the Brookings Institution's William Gale and Andrew Samwick wrote in a 2014 paper. Well-designed tax policy can increase growth, they wrote, but to do so, tax cuts have to come alongside spending cuts.

And even then, it can't just be any spending cuts—it has to be cuts to "unproductive" spending.

"I want to be clear—one can write down models where taxes generate big effects," Gale told NPR. But models are not the real world, he added. "The empirical evidence is quite different from the modeling results, and the empirical evidence is much weaker."

It's not just Gale. According to a 2012 report from the nonpartisan Congressional Research Service (referenced by the *New York Times'* David Leonhardt in a 2012 column), top marginal tax rates and economic growth have not appeared correlated over the past 60 years. One other nuance—it depends on the type of tax cut. You can imagine how cutting taxes for lower earners might boost activity more than cutting the top marginal rate—lower-income Americans with an extra $100 are more likely to spend that money than a millionaire.

Likewise, the economic research firm Moody's found in 2008 that temporary tax cuts (like rebates) could boost GDP, but permanent ones had a much weaker effect. Meanwhile, boosting spending on programs like food stamps and unemployment had a stronger effect, they found.

In short, if your sole, ultimate goal is faster growth, tax cuts might not be the best policy.

Why It Matters, Part 1: What do these plans cost?

This might seem like a stupid question—*of course economic growth matters!*—but it matters doubly for these tax plans because it affects how much they end up costing. And most of the Republicans' plans look really, really expensive.

A lot of the conversation about revenue in this week's debate focused on estimates from the Tax Foundation, a right-leaning tax policy think tank in Washington, D.C., that has scored many of the GOP candidates' tax plans.

That group releases what are called static and dynamic scores. Dynamic scores are complicated: They take into account potential economic effects—for example, they assume that tax cuts can generate economic growth and therefore, revenue. Static scores are much simpler, ignoring those effects.

And that's a weakness of static scores—policies have effects. But dynamic scores involve the impossible task of predicting the future. A perfect dynamic score would be the best option, but no one knows

how to do a perfect dynamic score. So dynamic scores are inherently uncertain as well, and there are a lot of ways to get them wrong.

To see this fight in action, look back to earlier this year, when the Congressional Budget Office, with a new GOP-appointed director, announced it would start issuing dynamic scores.

Or look at the Tax Foundation. Many (Gale included) say the group's dynamic scores are too generous, making policies like tax cuts look cheaper than they really are.

And here's where the bottom line comes in—even if you do believe the Tax Foundation's dynamic scores are way too generous, as of earlier this month, they found that one candidate (Rand Paul) comes out with a plan that won't slash revenue, while most of the other candidates will cut it by more than $1 trillion over 10 years.

Trump's plan, by this math, cuts revenue by $10 trillion over 10 years.

Why It Matters, Part II: How do you pay for it?

In that Chicago survey of economists, 71 percent either disagreed or strongly disagreed that tax cuts would lead to higher revenue in the next five years. Meanwhile, zero percent agreed that cutting taxes would raise revenue in the next five years.

"[A tax cut] won't pay for itself. You're not going to cut taxes by a dollar and get a dollar back in revenue from the growth," said Doug Holtz-Eakin, former director of the CBO.

In short, big revenue-cutting tax plans would have to come up with some big spending cuts. Marc Goldwein, senior vice president at the Committee for a Responsible Federal Budget, uses Gov. Jeb Bush's tax plan as an example.

"Gov. Bush's tax cut is between $1 and $4 trillion," Goldwein said. "He's making his job that much harder when not only does he have to reduce the debt but also he's got to pay for his tax cuts first."

Ben Carson's tax plan, for example, appears to leave a $2 trillion gap between spending and revenue, according to math from CNBC debate moderator Becky Quick this week (and Carson's math—in which he seemed to say he would somehow tax all of GDP, not just income—is not how taxes currently work).

For its part, the Carson campaign tells NPR that all will eventually be revealed.

"We expect to issue our tax plan in a few weeks, then all your questions and those of Ms. Quick will be ably answered," campaign spokesman Doug Watts wrote back. "We are not going to piecemeal answers because we continue to refine the details, which will be professionally scored and prove Ms. Quick wrong."

"[Lower revenue] means they must be claiming they're willing to fix it on the other side of the budget," Holtz-Eakin said. "Show me how you're going to do that."

He argues that tax plans can't be viewed in isolation; a tax plan that cuts revenue should simply come alongside other plans that cut spending.

Or maybe we're taking candidates' tax plans too seriously.

"I don't think they're realistic, but I don't think that's the real way to indict them," he added. "They're campaign plans. They're never like legislation."

Candidates are presenting their dream worlds of fiscal policy, he says—the way the US would operate if they could get everything they wanted through Congress (which won't happen).

Viewed this way, different campaigns appear to be saying different things: Marco Rubio wants families with kids to have more income. Bush and Paul, for their parts, are aiming for more business investment and growth. And so on.

Then again, this is also kind of a disappointing idea—if voters aren't supposed to read tax plans as, well, tax plans, what incentive do campaigns have to make them into serious-looking proposals?

The Short Answer:
Candidates tend to oversimplify the relationship between tax cuts and economic growth.

EVALUATING THE AUTHOR'S ARGUMENTS:

Viewpoint author Danielle Kurtzleben references a study by the Congressional Research Service that found that over the last sixty years, there has been no correlation between top tax rates and economic growth. If that's the case, why do you think Republican presidential candidates are so eager to cut the top marginal tax rate?

The Government Goes Too Far with the Social Cost of Carbon

Roger Bezdek and Paul Driessen

"America's policies, laws and regulations [should] recognize the critical importance and benefits of carbon-based fuels to the nation's economic growth and job creation."

In the following viewpoint, Roger Bezdek and Paul Driessen assail the Obama administration's implementation of the social cost of carbon metric (SCC). The authors argue that increased atmospheric CO_2 is, in fact, beneficial for several reasons—reasons that have been refuted. Ultimately, they believe that unfathomable technological advances make it irresponsible for scientists to model climate changes for the next three hundred years and that the government should eliminate the SCC and all policies, accords, legislation, and funding related to climate change. Bezdek runs a consulting firm that works with the energy industry. Driessen is a lobbyist.

AS YOU READ, CONSIDER THE FOLLOWING QUESTIONS:
1. What is the Social Cost of Carbon (SCC)?
2. How, according to the authors, does an increase in atmospheric CO_2 relate to food production?
3. What do the authors believe is the indirect benefit of CO_2?

The SCC scheme attempted to curb harmful environmental pollutants.

The Obama Administration aggressively used a Social Cost of Carbon (SCC) scheme to justify federal regulations pertaining to carbon-based fuels, carbon dioxide and methane emissions, coal mine and pipeline permit denials, energy development foreign aid, and many other actions.

While "SCC" may sound esoteric or academic, it is a critical concept. Without the artificial and inflated SCC estimates, many recent energy and environmental regulations could not have been justified or promulgated.

As a first priority, the Trump Administration must review, revise, reject or even rescind the SCC, and reduce its values well below what Obama used—perhaps even to zero or negative numbers. Doing so will destroy the justification for many expensive, intrusive, punitive, useless, counterproductive regulations.

[...]

In simplest terms, the SCC is an estimate of the monetized damages associated with an incremental increase in carbon emissions in a given year. It is meant to be a comprehensive estimate of climate change damages and of how much society would supposedly gain by slashing fossil fuel use and CO_2 emissions.[1]

The purpose of the SCC estimates is to allow agencies to incorporate the social benefits of reducing CO_2 emissions into benefit-cost analyses of regulatory actions. The Environmental Protection Agency and other federal agencies use the SCC to estimate the asserted climate benefits of their rulemakings.

The new, higher SCC estimates were used for the first time in a June 2013 rule on efficiency standards for microwave ovens.[2] These SCC estimates, prepared with little publicity, debate, or public input, have ominous implications for the US economy, consumers, and especially its manufacturing sectors.

Fundamental SCC Problems

Using this social cost of carbon format in benefit-cost analysis and proposed rulemakings entails at least three major deficiencies.

First, and most fundamentally, the SCC is based on the thesis, assertion, or alleged "consensus" that manmade carbon dioxide is the primary force controlling global warming and climate change—and that solar, cosmic ray, oceanic, and other powerful forces now play only minor, inconsequential roles.

In reality, as climatologist Judith Curry notes, within the scientific community there are still "MASSIVE uncertainties" about the climate system, including the degree to which a doubling of atmospheric CO_2 levels will affect global temperatures; how the overall carbon cycle works; the complex interplay of numerous natural forces; the degree to which human activities and energy use affect these processes (locally, regionally and globally); and the notable inability thus far of climate models to predict global temperatures, extreme weather events, regional climate changes, and sea level rise.[3]

Second, the methodology used by the IWG in developing the SCC estimates is not rigorous; indeed, it is flexible enough to produce almost any estimates and outcomes the IWG or its agency members might desire, especially over the three-century period (!) for which they are claiming to forecast.

Third, and more serious, no attempt is made to estimate (or even acknowledge the existence of) the many benefits, or positive externalities, of using carbon-based fuels and emitting carbon dioxide.

[...]

Parameters of Benefit-Cost Analysis

There are two types of carbon benefits that must be identified, analyzed and, to the degree possible, quantified: direct benefits and indirect benefits.

The major *direct* carbon benefit—or more accurately, the direct *carbon dioxide* benefit—is to increase agricultural productivity. In addition to increasing the *quantity* of food available for human consumption, the rising atmospheric CO_2 concentration is also improving the *quality* of our foods, the speed at which crops grow, their ability to withstand prolonged arid or drought conditions, and even their ability to resist disease. Similar benefits accrue to natural habitats: forests, grasslands, and phytoplankton.[4]

Even more important, the *indirect* benefits of carbon include the immense value to modern economies and societies of affordable, reliable energy produced by carbon-based fuels. These fuels have literally created modern technological societies worldwide, improved living standards for billions of people on the planet, increased life spans by decades, and over the past 20 years alone lifted over a billion persons out of abject poverty. They are simply invaluable and irreplaceable, and will remain so for the foreseeable future.

[...]

Indirect Benefits of CO_2 and Fossil Fuels

The relationship between world Gross Domestic Product (GDP) and carbon dioxide emissions over the past century is strong. It is clear that, at present, fossil fuels—from which CO_2 is an essential byproduct, along with water vapor—are creating $60–$70 trillion in annual global GDP.

[…]

Instead of bemoaning alleged costs of carbon, the Obama agencies should have been extolling the unprecedented benefits of using fossil fuels and emitting carbon dioxide.

[…]

Obama SCC: More Problems

Government SCC modelers claim they can accurately forecast global temperature and climate, weather, human population, technological advances, economic development, living standards—and damages to the world's civilizations and ecosystems from US carbon dioxide emissions—for the next 300 years!

Even without considering the numerous uncertainties over natural and manmade climate change during the coming centuries, or the preceding analysis, it is clear that this claim is ridiculous and indefensible.

[…]

No one living in 1717 could have foreseen even steam engines or ironclad warships 150 years later. Just 125 years back in time, Wisconsin's Hearthstone House became the world's first home lit by hydroelectric power—and nary a soul could have predicted the scope of household or business reliance on electrical power today.

Just 70 years ago, at the end of World War II, computers, plastics, jet airplanes, air travel, nuclear power and even telephones were in their infancy—and no one could foresee how far they would advance by 2017. A mere 35 years ago, laptop computers, the internet, digital photography, cell phones, fracking and other technologies so commonplace today did not exist, and not one IWG modeler could have envisioned them.

Today the pace of change is exponential. And yet government SCC modelers claim they can prophesy technologies and carbon/carbon dioxide costs to humanity and planet over the next 300 years—while still not considering the incredible benefits of fossil fuels and plant-fertilizing CO_2 emissions. Even more preposterous, they insist that their soothsaying should be the basis for today's energy and economic policies and laws, which would put the entire US economy under the control of regulators, pressure groups and crony corporate interests that would profit from their decisions, subsidies and mandates.

This is junk science, Garbage In–Garbage Out modeling, phony forecasting, and calculated deception perhaps bordering on fraud. Obama-era social cost of carbon must not be a foundation for policymaking.

Conclusions

What specifically should the White House and Congress do?

1) Reframe and revise the social cost of carbon process, by demonstrating the absurdity and falsity of what the Obama Interagency Working Group and its agency members attempted to do.

2) Emphasize the demonstrable, observable, incredible benefits of carbon-based fuels and increased atmospheric carbon dioxide— and explain how those benefits clearly outweigh any hypothesized costs by 50:1, 500:1 or more, now and for at least the next several decades.

3) Revise, rescind, and defund policies and regulations that were based on the old SCC analysis, beginning with the "endangerment" rule, Clean Power Plan, Climate Action Plan, and all domestic and overseas use of the SCC and "dangerous manmade climate change" to justify decisions on oil, natural gas, coal, fracking, methane leakage, pipelines, renewable energy programs and subsidies, foreign aid, the Paris climate agreement, and many other actions.[5]

4) Drastically reduce or terminate any US financial contributions to the UN Framework Convention on Climate Change (UNFCCC), Intergovernmental Panel on Climate Change, Green Climate Fund, and similar programs—at least until they are dramatically reformed in accord with the emerging and growing recognition that we still know very little about the causes, implications and possible adaptive measures for climate change, or the totality of costs and benefits or carbon fuels and carbon dioxide emissions.

5) Finally, extricate the United States from the terms, obligations, and impediments of the Paris Climate Agreement, by presenting it to the US Senate under the Constitution's "advice and consent" clause, on the ground that it is clearly and legally a treaty requiring two-thirds ratification, and does not qualify as a mere agreement or presidential executive order. Alternatively, do so by withdrawing the United States from the original 1992 UN Framework Convention on Climate Change, thereby absolving the USA from any further energy, economic or financial commitments under international climate treaties.

These actions will help establish honest and defensible benefit-cost analyses for the nation's deliberative process—and restore sound, replicable science to the global warming and climate change debate. Equally important, they will help ensure that America's policies, laws and regulations recognize the critical importance and benefits of carbon-based fuels to the nation's economic growth and job creation (and of carbon dioxide for its agriculture and ecosystems) for decades to come.

Endnotes

1. Interagency Working Group on Social Cost of Carbon, United States Government, "Technical Support Document: Technical Update of the Social Cost of Carbon for Regulatory Impact Analysis Under Executive Order 12866," May 2013; Interagency Working Group on Social Cost of Carbon, United States Government, "Technical Support Document: Social Cost of Carbon for Regulatory Impact Analysis Under Executive Order 12866," February 2010.
2. US Department of Energy, "Energy Conservation Program: Energy Conservation Standards for Standby Mode and Off Mode for Microwave Ovens," 10 CFR Parts 429 and 430.
3. Judith Curry, "Rethinking the Social Cost of Carbon: The social cost of carbon is emerging as a major source of contention in the Trump Administration," JudithCurry.com, January 17, 2017, https://judithcurry.com/2017/01/17/rethinking-the-social-cost-of-carbon/
4. See Paul Driessen, *Miracle Molecule: Carbon dioxide, gas of life* (foreword by Dr. Roy Spencer), a CFACT eBook available through Amazon.com and BarnesAndNoble.com (2014).
5. For scholarly articles on climate change rulings, see Timothy Benson, The Heartland Institute, "Comments, petitions and testimony opposing EPA's CO2 endangerment finding (January 18, 2017).

EVALUATING THE AUTHORS' ARGUMENTS:

The crux of the viewpoint authors' argument is that the future is so full of unknowns it's foolish to try to make plans. Is this a compelling enough argument against efforts to protect the environment, even if future discoveries and technological advances may change the relationship between humankind and climate change?

With the Social Cost of Carbon, the Government Recognizes Its Moral Imperative

John Wihbey

"'There are ethics involved.' It very much comes down to 'how we value future generations.'"

In the following viewpoint, John Wihbey analyzes the moral and regulatory significance of the social cost of carbon (SCC). SCC is not a tax; it is a quantification that allows the government to measure the socially detrimental effect of CO_2 production when it goes about enacting rules and regulations. Moreover, it gives the government's decision making a moral imperative, because, as one expert is quoted, "It's not just wonky cost-benefit. It's what our grandchildren would want us to do." Wihbey is an assistant professor of journalism at Northeastern University.

AS YOU READ, CONSIDER THE FOLLOWING QUESTIONS:
1. What is the current dollar value of the social cost of carbon?
2. How many government agencies and offices helped devise SCC?
3. In how many rulemaking scenarios does SCC encourage a different regulation?

T he social cost of carbon—"SCC," as it's known. Sounds a bit wonky. Yet it is becoming a crucial new instrument in putting a "price on carbon," even as for many its meaning remains elusive, hard to grasp.

"It's the most important figure you've never heard of," says economist Michael Greenstone, a key architect of the concept as Chief Economist of President Obama's Council of Economic Advisors.

The EPA defines it as "an estimate of the economic damages associated with a small increase in carbon dioxide (CO_2) emissions, conventionally one metric ton, in a given year." The dollar figure assigned, then, "represents the value of damages avoided for a small emission reduction (i.e. the benefit of a CO_2 reduction)." The current dollar value is $37 per ton of carbon dioxide emitted.

Greenstone, now director of the Energy Policy Institute at the University of Chicago, hastens to add, "It's not just wonky cost-benefit. It's what our grandchildren would want us to do."

The figure, in other words, has a unique moral dimension. So perhaps, then, it's our moral duty to understand it.

Connecting Social Costs to Our Own Lives

The government now has a specific number it can use to make rule changes, taking into account economic damages as a result of climate change. If policy X—let's say, a rule allowing the expansion of a power plant—prevents the generation of millions of tons of carbon dioxide, multiply those tons by $37 to get the value of damages avoided by the rule. That number is then counted as a net social benefit.

Grasping the true meaning of giant, industrial-size dollar figures can be difficult. But there's a simple way to think about it, based on a little back-of-the-envelope calculation:

America's overreliance on cars has a measurable draining effect on society.

- The activities of every American right now produce about 18 tons of carbon dioxide per year.
- About one-third of that, let's say six tons, comes from transportation.
- So multiply six by $37, and you get $222. That's how much the daily commute, rides to the grocery store and road trips—all our carbon-producing travel—cost in societal damages each year.

Valuing Future Generations

Perhaps, however, you agree with Stanford researchers Frances C. Moore and Delavane B. Diaz and think it's likely much higher (their recently published $220/ton figure means our commuting-to-work damages, etc., are somewhere around $1,320 each year). Some environmental groups have long been advocating for an even higher figure—$266/ton, and more.

Reasonable people can certainly disagree—even by orders of magnitude, according to the National Research Council. "There's no right answer.... I think it's almost for regular people to decide, as opposed to people in the ivory tower," says Joseph Aldy, an environmental economist at Harvard who was Special Assistant to the President for Energy and Environment in the Obama White House.

"There are ethics involved," he said in a recent interview. It very much comes down to "how we value future generations"—not an easy concept to pin down.

But the ultimate goal, Greenstone said in an interview, is to make climate change decision-making more "garden variety" and less emotional: "This is an economic decision at the end of the day."

It may seem arbitrary to some for the government to put a precise value on something so squishy as collective societal damage from climate change, but it's increasingly common to try to proceed in this way. Government regulators long have put the statistical value of a human life at about $9 million. They have calculated the value of building more bathrooms as part of efforts to prevent prison rapes, and calculated the value of requiring cameras in vehicles' rear-view mirrors to protect small children.

Origins and Applications

Under President Ronald Reagan, the government mandated that new regulations need to undergo a cost-benefit analysis. But damages resulting from greenhouse gas emissions were not being taken into account in those calculations, and a 2008 federal appeals court decision ordered executive agencies to begin doing so. Officials such as Greenstone and regulatory "czar" Cass Sunstein—then the head of the Office of Management and Budget's Office of Information and Regulatory Affairs—convened an interagency working group and began hammering out a figure.

SCC is the product of the combined efforts of 12 government offices or agencies. They arrived at a "mainstream" working figure—kind of the middle of a range—to be updated occasionally, to evaluate proposed rules. It takes into account predicted changes in economic growth and some physical impacts, such as the potential for increased flooding and property damage, diminished human health, and agricultural productivity loss. But the possibilities of catastrophes and tipping points don't really play a role in its formulation. (When

Congressional Republicans questioned how it was developed, the Government Accountability Office investigated and in 2014 found that it was arrived at honestly.)

But how exactly has it been put into practice?

An example: EPA and the Department of Transportation had to do a cost-benefit analysis for light-duty vehicles. Technology costs for companies to raise fuel efficiency standards were estimated at $350 billion over four decades. Benefits to society—for example, reduced pollution and congestion, and more energy security—were pegged at $280 billion. So higher fuel efficiency standards don't pass muster: They are $70 billion in the "red." Yet once the social costs of carbon are taken into account, cost-benefit analysis showed net benefits of more than $100 billion. Now the higher standards and new rules can move forward.

The figure first came to real public attention in 2013, when it was applied to new rules for microwave ovens. That rule showed that government regulators had raised the price from about $24 a ton to its current level.

Its impact has not been overwhelming—yet. In a 2014 working paper for the Brookings Institution, researchers Robert W. Hahn of Oxford University and Robert A. Ritz of Cambridge University looked at the net benefits involved in 53 regulatory policies. It turns out that the social cost of carbon is low enough that it typically means only 14 percent of net benefits from a policy are accounted for by reducing carbon; and weighing the social cost of carbon tipped the scales in favor of a different policy in only about 1 in every eight rule-making scenarios.

Hahn and Ritz note that "in almost all cases, estimated net benefits are positive both with and without the social cost of carbon." For SCC to really "bite," in other words, it will need to be applied in many more cases across American economic activity, and the figure may need to be much bigger. It has nowhere near the power of a carbon tax, a cap-and-trade scheme, or any other true, systematic "price on carbon."

Are You a 1-, 3-, 5- or 7-Percenter?

The government uses three different models from the peer-reviewed literature to achieve a diverse analysis (they call them "IAMs," or integrated assessment models), and then synthesizes them into a range of figures. The most important thing to keep in mind is that the calculations very much come down to the "discount rate," a statistical term that refers to how we value something into the future—in this case, avoiding the release of a ton of carbon into the atmosphere.

Journalists and policymakers alike have attempted valiantly to break down and simplify the discount rate concept for the public. It's worth just knowing that those favoring aggressive action on climate change now might fall into the 2.5 or 3 percent camp, or even lower. That means the value right now for avoiding a ton of carbon emissions is pretty high. (The famous "Stern Review" of 2007 had an even lower discount rate of about 1.4 percent.) Or, if you think avoiding more emissions in the short term is not as valuable, you'd fall into the 5 or 7 percent camp, or higher. The government runs all those scenarios, but the 3 percent is one that is generally used.

Groups such as the Environmental Defense Fund (EDF) and the Natural Resources Defense Council (NRDC) say that the current $37 figure neglects a vast range of negative impacts. Even updating the current models won't help that much, they say, as they are too narrow in focus.

Sunstein himself, who helped oversee SCC's creation, notes predictable divisions across government agencies. As he wrote in a recent paper, "It would not be terribly surprising to find that the Council of Economic Advisers and the National Economic Council, drawing on standard economic thinking, favor something in the range of a 5 percent rate, while the Environmental Protection Agency and the Council on Environmental Quality, influenced by critiques of that thinking and highly attentive to the interests of future generations ... favor a lower rate."

The University of Chicago's Greenstone says that there has been an "explosion" of research on the economic impacts of climate change in recent years, none yet factored into the current models. He's working with experts at several other academic institutions to formulate an updated model. Aldy notes that, so far, researchers and policymakers have "not done a good job" bridging the hard science and climate modeling and the economic impact scholarship.

Heading into another presidential election season—where the future of this important, emerging regulatory tool may hang in the balance—many policymakers and academics are eager to enshrine, at the very least, a more regular process for revisiting and revising the figure in the future. Providing some predictability in an area of such uncertainty, they say, is the least we can do for future generations.

EVALUATING THE AUTHOR'S ARGUMENTS:

Based on viewpoint author John Wihbey's evaluation of SCC, do you believe the government should apply SCC to a larger segment of the American economy?

Chapter 3

Is It Time to Rethink Taxes?

There must be a better way to deal with taxes.

For a Just Society, Start with Taxes

Alan Carter and Stephen Matthews

"Tax policy can play a major role in making the post-tax income distribution less unequal."

In the following viewpoint, Alan Carter and Stephen Matthews consider the ways in which strategic changes to the tax code could help right income inequality for the thirty-five member states of the Organisation for Economic Co-operation and Development (OECD). Raising taxes on top earners won't do much to redistribute wealth, they say. Instead, they're in favor of targeted taxation, such as increases to the tax rates for residential property and of closing loopholes. They also urge the implementation of sophisticated IT systems designed to root out tax evaders. Carter is head of international tax dialogue secretariat at the OECD. Matthews is chief tax economist at the OECD.

AS YOU READ, CONSIDER THE FOLLOWING QUESTIONS:
1. What does the Gini coefficient measure?
2. In most developed nations, what percentage of the GDP comes from tax revenue?
3. By how many percentage points have top marginal tax rates in OECD nations fallen from 1981 to 2010?

"How Tax Can Reduce Inequality," by Alan Carter and Stephen Matthews, OECD Observer No 290-291, Q1-Q2, 2012. http://oecdobserver.org/news/fullstory.php/aid/3782/How_tax_can_reduce_inequality.html.

Many experts agree that tax reform can help reduce income inequality.

The rapid growth of emerging economies in the past decade or so has lifted hundreds of millions of people out of absolute poverty and reduced income disparities across the world as a whole. At the same time, until the financial and economic crisis of 2008, most other economies were expanding too. However, within the OECD and emerging economies not all regions or people benefitted equally from the growth years. On the contrary, the distribution of income tended to become more unequal.

Unsurprisingly, particularly since the onset of the crisis, these trends have increased the salience of "fairness" in political debate in many countries, in terms of both equality of opportunity and of outcomes for household incomes and consumption. While few doubt that fairness is important, interpretations of what is fair differ and may in part reflect historical norms for the distribution of income, which can differ widely between countries. That said, over the longer term too much inequality may be inimical to growth.

The Potential for Tax Policy

Tax policy can play a major role in making the post-tax income distribution less unequal. In addition, tax policy is crucial for raising revenues to finance public expenditure on transfers, health and education that tend to favour low-income households, as well as on growth-enabling infrastructure that can also increase social equity.

Inequality tends to be less pronounced in OECD countries than elsewhere in the world, though in recent decades the distribution of disposable incomes has tended to become more unequal. In the mid-1980s the Gini coefficient, whereby 0 is perfectly equal (and the higher the coefficient, the more unequal is a distribution) stood at 0.28 among the working-age population, on average, in OECD countries. By the mid-2000s it had become more unequal, increasing to 0.31.

What then are the implications for tax policy? Work by the OECD experts and many others on tax reform and economic growth stress the need to weigh up the extent to which high marginal tax rates on income can act as a disincentive, for instance, for investment in human capital or discourage entrepreneurship, and the fact that progressive taxation of income is one of the main ways for governments to redistribute incomes. For many countries the potential trade-offs between economic growth objectives and equity are particularly critical at present.

The effects of taxation on income distribution needs to be seen in the context of the trade-offs between growth and equity, and this means looking at the overall effects of any reform on the fiscal regime as a whole, and not just at whether individual taxes are progressive or regressive. This is because the distribution of disposable incomes depends on both taxes and benefits. Raising indirect taxes, for instance, is often regressive where these taxes fall on the consumption of goods and services that make up a larger share of the budgets of poorer than richer households. But the overall impact of a fiscal reform can still be progressive, if these effects are offset by other tax and benefit changes. Income-related benefits, for example, are a much more efficient way of increasing the disposable income of poorer households than reduced rates of VAT.

Nor is VAT necessarily bad for redistribution. This is clear in the case of developing countries, where the relatively greater reliance on indirect taxes may make their tax systems more regressive. On the other hand, consumption taxes such as VAT may be the only way to finance (more) strongly progressive spending. However, as some countries lack the administrative capacity to make welfare transfers to households, there may be a case for differentiating VAT rate structures to tax "necessities" at a lower rate, if at all.

Most developed countries already have well-developed tax regimes that raise, on average, tax revenues equivalent to some 35% of GDP. The scale of tax revenues is capable of achieving a significant amount of redistribution. However, it is also capable, if structural tax policies are poorly designed, of becoming detrimental to economic performance.

Lowering Taxes: Back to the 1980s

During the 1980s a number of countries became concerned that high marginal tax rates were one of the factors that had contributed to the slowdown in economic growth in many countries in the 1970s. Moreover, high tax rates were encouraging the development of selective tax reliefs, which distorted investment decisions, and extensive (even aggressive) tax planning through the exploitation of loopholes that narrowed the tax base. Reformers decided to adopt a "broad base-low rate" approach instead, which meant pushing down statutory rates of both corporate and personal income taxes, and recovering potentially lost revenue by applying these tax rates to a broader base.

The apparent success of such reforms encouraged others to emulate them. Moreover, competitive pressures arising from the effects of liberalising trade and financial flows (notably growing international integration and globalisation) also put downward pressures on tax rates. Top marginal statutory rates of personal tax, in particular, have been cut quite substantially in many cases, from an OECD average of 66.8% in 1981 to 41.7% in 2010.

Faced with the challenge of how to restore sustainable public finances and the growth of output and employment following the post-2008 recession, what tax policies should OECD countries pursue now? Can tax policies be devised that will be perceived to be "fair" and help maintain the social cohesion, while supporting growth too? Where additional tax revenues have to be raised as part of fiscal consolidation plans, can this be achieved by broadening tax bases to make more of the income of better-off individuals taxable, or should marginal statutory tax rates be raised too?

Simply raising marginal personal income tax rates on high earners will not necessarily bring in much additional revenue, because of effects on work intensity, career decisions, tax avoidance and other behavioural responses. Where tax increases are necessary, the most growth-friendly approach would be to reduce tax-induced distortions that harm growth, including closing loopholes, and to raise more revenues from recurrent taxes on residential property, while setting taxes to reduce environmental damage and correct other externalities.

As ever, the devil is in the detail, but there are a number of ways in which such reforms could contribute to social equity. For instance, many tax breaks favour higher income individuals disproportionately. The case for reviewing their effectiveness is clearly compelling.

There is also scope to raise taxation of residential property which is relatively lightly taxed in many countries. However, while the better off tend to own the most expensive residential property, there are many middle class owners too, so reform has to be approached cautiously, especially given the bruising many home-owners took from the housing bubble. Nevertheless, out-of-date values for tax purposes often distort the efficiency of property markets (by discouraging individuals from moving home, thus reducing labour mobility) and many existing property taxes tend to be regressive, i.e. take proportionally more of the income of poorer households. Reform and revaluation could make property taxes both fairer and less distortive.

Good tax administration also matters. New IT systems in use in revenue administrations increasingly include tools such as sophisticated risk engines to identify potential missing revenues. Efforts to curb offshore non-compliance by making the exchange of information among tax authorities more effective have been given a new impetus. Tax evaders, who are often wealthy, have fewer places to hide their money. These initiatives also bolster international efforts by the IMF, OECD, UN and World Bank to help low-income countries to develop more effective tax systems.

In short, tax reform can promote more equity while unblocking growth, so that the next rising tide lifts more boats together.

EVALUATING THE AUTHORS' ARGUMENTS:

Nordic nations have higher taxes than the United States. They also provide health care, exemplary education, maternal and paternal leave, and other social services to its citizens. They do this based on what is sometimes called the "Nordic Theory of Love." The idea is that higher taxes can actually liberate citizens because, for example, you don't have to take a job you don't want just so you can have health insurance. What do you make of this argument for taxes?

Paying Taxes and Giving to Charity Aren't the Same Thing

Mark Rosenman

"The notion that the wealthy will pay out in voluntary contributions what they don't pay in mandatory taxes may seem an attractive proposition, but it just isn't so."

The very wealthy sometimes claim that paying taxes is a form of charity. Some have gone so far as to argue that if the income tax were eliminated, charitable contributions would pick up the slack. Mark Rosenman makes a strong case against that way of thinking in the following viewpoint. The author asserts that safety and welfare has and always will be under the government's domain. One role of government is to protect the common good, and neither charitable organizations nor wealthy individuals can fill those shoes. Rosenman is professor emeritus at the Union Institute and University and director of Caring to Change.

AS YOU READ, CONSIDER THE FOLLOWING QUESTIONS:

1. What is the relationship between taxes and "the price of giving"?
2. What sort of nonprofit organizations do the wealthy favor?
3. What 1990 book by Teresa Odendahl helped inspire a wave of charitable giving?

"Paying Taxes and Giving to Charity Aren't the Same Thing," by Mark Rosenman, the Chronicle of Philanthropy, September 4, 2012. Reprinted by permission.

Studies have found that charity donations would not necessarily increase if taxes were less burdensome on citizens.

Some of the wealthiest Americans have started to contend that paying taxes and making charitable gifts are just about the same thing. Their failure to grasp the profound difference between the two presents a very real problem for nonprofit organizations and our democracy.

Mitt Romney epitomized this thinking last January when he tacked charitable contributions onto his taxes while discussing the percentage of income reported and paid on his 2010 return. He used the same calculus again a few weeks ago while defending his record and his refusal to release past tax returns.

It quickly spread: Last month another multimillionaire took out a full-page ad in the national edition of the *New York Times* to oppose President Obama's tax proposals and said that "I realize paying taxes is a form of charitable giving in a sense." Affirming such conservative and libertarian thinking, a Cato Institute official also declared that "taxes are a form of charity."

Do Taxes Prohibit Charitable Giving?

Millionaires and other wealthy people argue that they would give more to charity if they paid lower taxes, as they surely would under proposals put forth by Mitt Romney and in the House-approved budget drafted by his running mate Paul Ryan.

That assertion is directly contradicted by scholarly studies. We know that when taxes go down, people give less generously. Lower taxes mean that what scholars call "the price of giving" goes up; the value of the tax deduction per donated dollar is less.

The notion that the wealthy will pay out in voluntary contributions what they don't pay in mandatory taxes may seem an attractive proposition to some charities, but it just isn't so.

While there may be more discretionary money in the pockets of millionaires, it tends to stay there. As a matter of fact, the wealthy give a smaller percentage of their income to charity than do moderate- and low-income people.

They also give to different charities than those with less income. The social psychologist Paul Piff, who studies the effects of income on personal behavior, told the *Chronicle* last month that "the more wealth you have, the more focused on your own self and your own needs you become and the less attuned to the needs of other people." He has shown that wealth can make people "more selfish, more insular, and less compassionate than other people."

Much of this has been known since 1990 when Terry Odendahl published *Charity Begins at Home*; wealthy Americans tend to support the nonprofit institutions that they themselves use. That includes elite universities, museums, operas, and performing-arts groups as well as other cultural institutions and some hospitals and medical facilities.

While such philanthropic activity is to be commended, few would consider these institutions to be on the frontline of charities dealing with today's most pressing problems.

Government's Role

And those problems are growing worse due to inadequate government funds. Parks, roads, and the power grid are deteriorating, while efforts to improve schools, assure food safety, slow the shrinking of the middle class, alleviate poverty, protect the environment, care for animals, and deal with myriad other issues are all hampered by the money squeeze facing governments at every level.

While charitable support can and should be directed to solve these critical social, environmental, and economic challenges, it cannot and ought not be seen as a replacement for government. We established government to hold enduring responsibility for America's public safety and welfare.

It is government that has the ability, through our democratically elected representatives, to identify and analyze threats to Americans' safety and welfare, to set priorities, and to propose and adopt appropriate responses. It is only government—at the federal, state, and local levels—that has the legitimate power appropriate to these tasks. And government must have the authority to secure the money needed to carry out its jobs.

Neither civil society nor the market can fulfill the role of government. Donors can decide to support anything they want, and they should—but they are not obligated to look out for the common good in the way we demand of elected representatives.

By claiming that they should be able to make voluntary charitable contributions rather than pay taxes is for the wealthy to demand the right to decide what is best for the rest of us. It is the wealthy placing themselves outside and above the public will. It is an elite demand for undue and illegitimate influence in the democratic process.

This does not serve the nation or charities well. The tax money being diverted to millionaires' pockets will quite likely not make it to charities' bank accounts, especially not to those of organizations that try to serve the needy.

In fact, the greed of millionaires who insist on lower taxes leads directly to the decline and actual decimation of government coffers to address myriad problems. That means that nonprofits will face growing needs of people and communities whose problems are made worse by declining government efforts at the same time that fewer government dollars are available to support charities' programs.

The leaders of charities, as well as everyone else who cares about the common good, need to challenge the notion that private avarice—no matter what the false promise of additional philanthropy—is no substitute for public responsibility.

EVALUATING THE AUTHOR'S ARGUMENTS:

The viewpoint author Rosenman argues that charities aren't able to protect the common good to the same extent as the government. Can you think of charitable endeavors that go beyond what the government alone is capable of?

Viewpoint

3

The Rich Should Pay Their Fair Share, but the Buffett Rule Is Not the Answer

"The idea of a tax code so riddled with loopholes that a billionaire could pay lower rates than his secretary quickly became a potent political symbol."

Steve Brooks

The Buffett Rule was a proposal by President Barack Obama that would have made 30 percent the minimum tax rate for anyone earning more than $1 million. In the following viewpoint, Steve Brooks argues that the Buffett Rule would not significantly generate tax revenue. He also notes that a similar system, the Alternative Minimum Tax, is already in place and doesn't work all that well. The author further contends that other initiatives, like an increase in the capital gains tax, would be a more effective way of making sure the wealthy pay their fair share. Brooks is an award-winning journalist whose work has appeared in *Fortune*, *BusinessWeek*, and the *Dallas Morning News*.

AS YOU READ, CONSIDER THE FOLLOWING QUESTIONS:
1. What is the Buffett Rule?
2. According to Senator Sheldon Whitehouse, how much tax revenue would the Buffett Rule generate?
3. What are capital gains?

Raise my taxes, please!

That was the request of Warren Buffett, the 81-year-old CEO of Berkshire Hathaway and the third-richest man in the world. In August 2011 he penned a *New York Times* op-ed calling for higher taxes on millionaires like himself.

Buffett's central claim was that for the most recent tax year, he paid lower rates than his employees, even though he earned millions more. "What I paid was only 17.4 percent of my taxable income," he wrote. "That's actually a lower percentage than was paid by any of the other 20 people in our office. Their tax burdens ranged from 33 percent to 41 percent and averaged 36 percent."

The idea of a tax code so riddled with loopholes that a billionaire could pay lower rates than his secretary quickly became a potent political symbol. President Barack Obama proposed the Buffett Rule: "No household making more than $1 million each year should pay a smaller share of their income in taxes than a middle class family pays."

An April bill by Sen. Sheldon Whitehouse (D-R.I.) would have levied a minimum tax of 30 percent on incomes over $2 million. Though the bill died in the Senate, an Associated Press/GfK Group poll found 60 percent of Americans favoring the rule and only 37 percent opposed. Even among Republicans, 43 percent backed the concept.

Economically Sound?

The Buffett Rule appears to make for good politics, but how does it rate in terms of economics?

Not so well, say tax and finance faculty at the University of Texas at Austin. "It's a political gimmick," says Robert Peroni, professor at

The "Buffett rule" is named for Warren Buffett, one of the nation's wealthiest men.

the School of Law. "I definitely think we need to reform our tax system, and that one aspect of that will be that many high-income people will be paying more in taxes than they are now." But the Buffett Rule, he argues, is a bad way to pursue a good goal.

He agrees that Buffett has shed light on a genuine problem. Although most millionaires pay higher tax rates than most middle-class earners, there are a significant number who don't. A March analysis of IRS data by the Congressional Research Service, found that 94,500 taxpayers with incomes over $1 million paid effective federal tax rates under 26.5 percent. Meanwhile, 10.4 million earners under $100,000 were paying rates over that figure.

Alternative Minimum Tax

So, why not sock a minimum tax on millionaires? The central problem, says Lillian Mills, accounting professor at the McCombs School of Business, is that one already exists. And both Democrats and Republicans agree it works poorly.

The Alternative Minimum Tax was first enacted in 1982, with a similar goal to the Buffett Rule: to root out rich tax dodgers. It requires them to calculate their incomes in two different ways—first for the standard income tax and again for the AMT—and pay the higher of the two taxes. The AMT strips away many popular deductions, trying to catch taxpayers who are loading up on loopholes.

"It adds a lot of complexity, when you have to figure your taxes in two different ways," says Mills. "This is a complexity that arose out of a lack of courage. Congress wanted to make sure that people who were claiming tax subsidies still paid a minimum amount of tax. But they didn't have the courage to just eliminate the subsidies."

Besides being complicated, the AMT has been catching many earners who aren't millionaires. That's because its income threshold was never indexed to rise with inflation. As Americans' incomes have risen, more and more middle-class families have crossed that threshold and become subject to the tax.

In recent years, Congress has repeatedly patched the AMT by temporarily raising its income thresholds. But the current patch expires at the end of this year. Without a new one, according to the Tax Policy Center, the AMT will strike 63 percent of married households with incomes between $75,000 and $100,000.

Add in the Buffett Rule on top of the AMT, and Americans would face three tax systems. "We already have one system that's a mess," says Peroni. "Let's not enact another one."

Besides, the extra tax revenue would barely make a dent in federal deficits. The congressional Joint Committee on Taxation estimated the Whitehouse bill would raise an extra $4.7 billion a year, while Whitehouse himself pegged it at $16 billion.

"If you cut federal spending 1 percent across the board, you would balance the budget a lot more than the Buffett Rule ever thought of doing," says Jim Nolen, a distinguished senior lecturer in finance who recently retired from McCombs.

Capital Gains

Instead of the Buffett Rule, there are more effective ways to prevent wealthy taxpayers from slipping through the cracks, say some professors. One is to raise tax rates on investment income.

Capital gains, which come from selling investments like stocks and real estate, are currently taxed at a top rate of 15 percent, compared to 35 percent for ordinary wages. The Congressional Budget Office reports that the top 0.01 percent of taxpayers get 44 percent of their income from capital gains and only 12 percent from wages. That's why investors like Buffett and Mitt Romney pay effective tax rates close to 15 percent.

Most economists say it's appropriate to tax capital gains more lightly, says Mills. "We tax them some, but not equal to earnings, driven by the economic theory that we don't want to discourage the investment that is the engine of our economy."

But the gap between wages and investments could be much narrower, without discouraging investment, says Peroni. He would raise the top capital gains rate to at least 20 percent.

But the most effective way to achieve Buffett's goals, he says, would be to repeal most of the deductions that have crept into the tax code since its last major overhaul, in 1986. Congress could then lower tax rates on everyone. Middle-class taxpayers would benefit the most, since they tend to take fewer and smaller deductions than wealthy ones.

"Let's get the basic income tax system correct," says Peroni. "We should be reforming income taxes across the board, not just focusing on the upper income levels. Let's see what people's taxable incomes are after these breaks are eliminated."

EVALUATING THE AUTHOR'S ARGUMENTS:

One could argue that while the Buffett Rule may not be a significant generator of tax revenue, it would serve as an important symbolic tax—a nod to the notion that the very wealthy are not, or cannot, avoid paying a reasonable share. Based on the arguments in Steve Brooks's viewpoint, do you agree or disagree with this notion of a symbolic tax?

The Progressive Tax Isn't Perfect, but the Flat Tax Isn't a Feasible Replacement

Glen Nunes

"There are advantages to both philosophies, and neither should be dismissed out of hand."

In the following viewpoint, Glen Nunes looks at the pros and cons of two tax systems that are much discussed: the flat income tax and the progressive income tax. In a flat tax system, all individuals pay the same tax rate. In a progressive system, an individual's tax rate is based on his or her income—the more he or she earns, the greater the percentage of his or her income that is taxable. Nunes reaches a pragmatic conclusion, arguing for a simpler tax code and the elimination of egregious loopholes. Nunes is a writer for ToughNickel.

AS YOU READ, CONSIDER THE FOLLOWING QUESTIONS:
1. On what group does a flat tax place increased burden?
2. What is "bracket creep"?
3. Why does the author believe the progressive tax is unconstitutional?

"Pros and Cons for the US of Flat vs. Progressive Taxes," by Glen Nunes, ToughNickel, April 21, 2016. Reprinted by permission.

Some suggest that a flat tax is the answer to economic growth.

Flat tax success stories are fairly easy to find. A number of countries have seen impressive economic growth after adopting the flat tax idea. This is especially true since the fall of the Soviet Union. As countries formerly under Soviet communist control adapted to capitalism, many of them made the flat tax part of their system and saw great economic growth. Would a flat tax be equally successful in the United States?

This article will discuss the definitions of flat and progressive taxation, looking at the pros and cons of each, and then speculate as to the effectiveness of the flat tax for the US.

Flat Tax Definition

At first glance, the flat tax idea seems simple enough: one tax rate, which applies to everyone, regardless of income. No deductions, loopholes or tax shelters—you multiply your income times the tax rate, and your taxes are done. Nothing could be easier!

In reality, it's not quite that simple. What constitutes income, for example? In the US, long-term capital gains are taxed at a lower rate than regular income, in part to encourage long-term investment. Should this continue under a flat tax plan?

Business income also complicates things, and not only for large corporations. If you have income from a small part-time business, for example, you currently deduct your expenses to determine the taxable amount. How would that work on a tax form that has no place to enter deductions? Clearly, business income requires additional rules.

Modified Flat Tax

A flat tax, applied across the board, would also increase the tax burden on those with lower incomes, many of whom currently pay little or no income tax. For all of these reasons, most current flat tax proposals are actually *modified* flat tax proposals. These modified plans usually include some variation of these elements:

- an income level beneath which no taxes are paid.
- a small number of allowable deductions—charitable contributions and home mortgage deductions are among the most common
- different rules, or at least different rates, for business income

Some "flat tax" plans also have a small number of tax brackets. Technically, this makes them progressive tax plans, although they are far "flatter" than our current system.

Flat Tax Pros and Cons
Pros

- easy to understand and comply with, thereby reducing errors and tax fraud

- professional tax preparers and advisors no longer needed, saving money for taxpayer
- lawmakers can no longer create tax loopholes in exchange for campaign contributions or other personal favors
- businesses can make decisions designed to better serve the marketplace and their stockholders, instead of trying to beat the tax code
- may encourage investment and expansion, as additional profit is not taxed at a higher rate

Cons

- may shift tax burden away from the rich, to the middle and lower class
- elimination of deductions may have negative impact on taxpayers with lower income
- government cannot use the tax code to encourage desirable activities, such as giving tax credits for making a home more energy-efficient
- thousands of government employees and tax professionals would lose their jobs, or suffer a large decrease in business
- effects on government revenue of converting to a flat tax are difficult to predict accurately

Progressive Tax Definition

A progressive tax is one in which the tax rate increases as income increases. In the US, this is done using tax brackets, in which income is divided into ranges, with each range taxed at a higher rate than the range below.

As a taxpayer's income enters a higher tax bracket, only the portion of income that falls into that bracket is taxed at the higher rate, with the remaining amount taxed according to the lower tax bracket(s) that it falls into. Otherwise, it would be theoretically possible for a person to earn more money but actually end up with less, due to the entire amount being taxed at the higher rate.

Progressive tax systems often allow for a number of adjustments to taxable income, such as exemptions, deductions, and tax credits.

These can be used to provide additional relief to low-income citizens, or to encourage certain types of behavior, such as business investment or higher education.

Progressive Tax Pros and Cons
Pros
- shifts tax burden to those most able to pay
- those with greater influence in society pay more
- prevents political and social instability by limiting the gap between classes (at least in theory)
- protects taxpayer during hard times—when income goes down, the tax rate also goes down
- many economists suggest that governments can get the most revenue from a progressive tax system

Cons
- "bracket creep"—inflation can push taxpayer into a higher tax bracket, with no real increase in income after adjusting for inflation
- can be used in corrupt manner by politicians
- "brain drain"—individuals with high earning potential (often a nation's brightest and most talented people) leave to avoid high taxes
- may discourage business investment and expansion, as additional profit is taxed at higher rates
- progressive taxation is arguably unconstitutional, in that it does not treat all citizens equally

Would Flat Tax Work in the US?
I've tried to accurately present the pros and cons of both flat and progressive taxation in an objective way. There are advantages to both philosophies, and neither should be dismissed out of hand. In my opinion, however, the flat tax is not the answer for the US.

First, there's no way of knowing how much of the economic growth seen in flat tax success stories are actually due to the flat tax.

Because of political changes and other economic reforms, many of these nations would have seen growth under almost any tax plan.

In addition, I'm not sure that a flat tax in the US could provide the same amount of revenue as the current tax system without increasing the tax burden on the middle class. Nor do I believe than anyone can predict the effects on the US economy of switching to a flat tax.

The workings of both the US economy and the current 11,000-page US tax code are extremely complicated. Anyone who says that they understand both well enough to accurately make predictions about the flat tax is, in my opinion, simply mistaken.

Simpler Tax

That uncertainty alone is reason enough not to switch to a flat tax —but this is not to say that there shouldn't be changes made. The current US tax code is *3.8 million words*. Compliance is difficult even for those who want to. Callers to the IRS with tax questions receive the wrong answer more than 20% of the time, according to the US Treasury.

Clearly, the US tax code needs to be vastly simplified. Progressive taxation is fine, but it should meet these criteria:

- everyone should actually pay the tax rate for their tax bracket— no loopholes, tax shelters, or other ways to avoid having to pay.
- it needs to be simple—an average citizen should not have to pay a professional to figure out how much he owes the government in taxes.
- the top tax rates should be low enough that they neither encourage "brain drain" nor stifle business investment.
- it should not be open to tinkering by politicians to use for their own ends.

It's also important to realize that taxes are only part of the equation. In the long run, no tax plan, flat or progressive, can help the US until the government learns not to spend more than it takes in.

EVALUATING THE AUTHOR'S ARGUMENTS:

The viewpoint author notes that if the United States shifted to a flat tax system, the government would no longer be able to encourage certain behaviors among taxpayers, like environmental consciousness, by offering tax breaks for activities like buying energy-efficient devices and electric cars. Should the government lose its ability to incentivize individuals in this way? Would you see it as a good or bad thing?

Facts About Taxes and Society

Editor's note: These facts can be used in reports to add credibility when making important points or claims.

- The first tax in the New World came about in 1619 when an early democratic body at Jamestown required that all men sixteen and older grow and harvest, for the government's benefit, ten pounds of tobacco.
- Taxation was a contentious issue among the Founding Fathers. Some, like Thomas Jefferson, were vehemently opposed, while others, like Alexander Hamilton, believed taxes were among the only ways for the fledgling nation to raise the revenue it would need to survive.
- During the tenure of President George Washington, the government enacted a tax on whiskey. This tax was so unpopular that, in 1794, it led to a militant uprising that Washington, at the helm of an army, had to quell. President Thomas Jefferson repealed the Whiskey Tax when he came into office.
- The nation was founded without an income tax. Instead, it relied on excise taxes on goods like alcohol and tobacco to generate federal capital. During the Civil War, however, Congress passed the Revenue Act of 1861, a national income tax of 3 percent on incomes greater than $800 per year in order to drum up revenue for the war effort. The tax was only temporary.
- In 1894, Congress passed the Wilson-Gorman Tariff Act, a 2 percent income tax. The next year, the Supreme Court ruled that the act was unconstitutional because the Constitution did not give Congress the authority to levy direct taxes that were not apportioned by state.
- The Sixteenth Amendment, which was ratified on February 3, 1913, amended the Constitution and gave Congress the power to levy direct taxes.

Taxes and Social Betterment

- In the wake of the Great Depression—as the top income tax rate rose from 25 percent to 79 percent—President Franklin Roosevelt created the Works Progress Administration (WPA). In just seven years, the WPA employed 8.5 million people to build 651,087 miles of road, 125,110 public buildings, and 8,192 parks.

- At the height of the Great Depression, 12,830,000 people were unemployed. In response, President Roosevelt created at least 100 "alphabet agencies" to protect workers and create jobs.

- Lasers, GPS, the internet—government funding, in one way or another, contributed to their discovery. From the 1960s through 2013, the federal government funded at least half of all basic scientific research in the country. Today, that number has fallen to 44 percent.

- In May 2013, President Donald Trump released a budget blueprint that called for the elimination of the National Endowment for the Arts (NEA). Conservative groups, like the Heritage Foundation, have long argued for disbanding the NEA. They believe the arts are well enough funded by philanthropy; that the NEA has, and will continue, to fund the production of art that some individuals may find lewd or offensive; and that the organization is wasteful. On the contrary, the NEA's $150 million budget is three times less than what the government spends on military bands. Moreover, the NEA has been instrumental in funding public memorials, such as the Vietnam Veterans Memorial; art museums, such as the Walker Art Center in Minneapolis; and pop culture sensations like *Hamilton.*

- In a 2017 interview, Paul Ryan, the speaker of the House, said he had been dreaming of cutting Medicaid, the national health care program for economically disadvantaged individuals that Congress established in 1965, since he was a college student "drinking at a keg." In Ryan's view, health care should "not [come] from the government." Instead, he and likeminded Republicans believe that the government should not be in the business of using tax dollars to pay for health care, welfare, or food stamps. In 2015, Medicaid provided health care for 97 million low-income Americans. Moreover, Medicaid costs 20 percent less than adult private insurance.

- As of 2015, there were 43.1 million people living in poverty, and 19.4 million in extreme poverty (earning less than $10,000 a year for a family of four).

- A survey from 2009 to 2012 found that 56 percent of Americans who use welfare services like Medicaid and food stamps did so for 36 months or fewer, undermining the argument that such programs create long-term dependencies.

- Those on the right in the US sometimes describe the country, disparagingly, as a "welfare state," one in which a portion of the population—too large a portion, as those disparagers would have it—relies on federal assistance—redirected tax dollars—for assistance. Etymologically, the notion of *welfare*, meaning social concern for the less fortunate, dates to 1904, but politically, in the US, its roots stretch even further back. As Kathryn J. Edin and H. Luke Shaefer explain in their book, *$2.00 a Day: Living on Almost Nothing in America*, welfare really began in the wake of the Civil War when states moved to established mother's aid programs to help newly widowed mothers keep their kids out of orphanages. The money for those programs ran out during the Great Depression, so President Roosevelt established Aid to Dependent Children (ADC). Though the program was far from perfect—it discriminated against unwed and African American mothers—by 1962 it served 3.6 million people. In the sixties, President Lyndon B. Johnson launched the War on Poverty, and over the next two decades, Medicare and Medicaid got going, the food stamps became permanent as did free school lunches, and by 1976 11.3 million Americans received cash assistance. But the 1980s saw a backlash against welfare, led by President Ronald Reagan. He called the War on Poverty a failure ("poverty won"). He peddled the story of a so-called welfare queen who had bilked the system for $150,000 a year. Increasingly, welfare attracted negative racial stereotypes. Politicians on either side of the political spectrum started calling for time limits and work requirements. Welfare was now most certainly a political issue, and an unpopular one at that, even though in 1994, two years before Congress passed the Personal Responsibility and Work Opportunity Reconciliation Act, fulfilling President Bill Clinton's pledge to "end welfare as we know it" by, among other things, instating a work requirement and killing the modern equivalent of the ADC, the number of Americans on welfare neared 15 million.

Taxes: The Rise and Fall

- According to the Tax Policy Center, in 2015 federal excise taxes raised $98.3 billion, roughly 3 percent of total tax revenue.
- In 1945, the top marginal tax rate was 94 percent. Today, it's 35 percent; though those in the top bracket often pay much less than that. Warren Buffett, the second richest man in the world, pays a lower tax rate than his secretary. Buffett, in turn, has called for a 30 percent minimum tax rate for those who make more than a million dollars a year.
- Proponents of trickle-down economics believe, as economist John Kenneth Galbraith wrote, "If you feed the horse enough oats, some will pass through to the road for the sparrows." In other words, economic benefits for the rich and powerful— lower taxes, corporate welfare—eventually benefit those who are lower down in the fiscal food chain. However, a study of 65 years of tax data found that cutting the top marginal tax rate did not yield economic growth but did increase income inequality.
- Thanks to a bevy of deductions and loopholes, those in the top 0.001 percent income bracket—meaning they make, at minimum, $62 million a year—pay a meager 17.60 percent tax rate, which is the same rate paid by someone making $85,000.
- US taxes account for 26 percent of the GDP, the fourth lowest among OECD nations.

Organizations to Contact

The editors have compiled the following list of organizations concerned with the issues debated in this book. The descriptions are derived from materials provided by the organizations. All have publications or information available for interested readers. The list was compiled on the date of publication of the present volume; the information provided here may change. Be aware that many organizations take several weeks or longer to respond to inquiries, so allow as much time as possible for the receipt of requested materials.

Center on Budget and Policy Priorities
820 First Street NE
Suite 510
Washington, DC 20002
(202) 408-1080
email: center@cbpp.org
website: www.cbpp.org
The Center on Budget and Policy Priorities is a nonpartisan research organization that pursues federal and state policies that reduce inequality and poverty. Taxation, particularly regarding programs and policies that help low-income people, is one of its primary areas of interest. The center applies its findings to inform debates and influence outcomes.

Guidestar
website: www.guidestar.org
Guidestar is a nonprofit organization that collects information, including tax filings, for other nonprofits across the United States. Guidestar's website includes a blog with informative articles aimed at helping to guide nonprofit organizations.

Institute on Taxation and Economic Policy
1616 P Street NW
Suite 200
Washington, DC 20036
(202) 299-1066
email: itep@itep.org
website: www.itep.org
The Institute on Taxation and Economic Policy's self-stated mission is to "ensure the nation has a fair and sustainable tax system that raises enough revenue to fund our common priorities, including education, health care, infrastructure and public safety."

National Priorities Project
351 Pleasant Street
Suite B, #442
Northampton, MA 01060
email: info@nationalpriorities.org
website: www.nationalpriorities.org
The National Priorities Project is a nonprofit, nonpartisan federal budget research organization. Its mission is to make the federal budget accessible to the public. The National Priorities Project provides the information, tools, and motivation that Americans need to understand the budget and develop strategies for taking fiscal action.

The Organisation for Economic Co-operation and Development (OECD)
2, rue André Pascal
75775 Paris Cedex 16
France
website: www.oecd.org
The Organisation for Economic Co-operation and Development (OECD) is a multinational organization aimed at improving the economic and social well-being of people around the world. The OECD works with governments to understand what drives social, economic, and environmental change and sets international standards on a wide range of things.

Tax Foundation
1325 G Street NW
Suite 950
Washington, DC 20005
(202) 464-6200
website: www.taxfoundation.org
The Tax Foundation is a nonprofit organization that conducts research and works to influence tax policy. This organization believes that an ideal tax code follows the principles of sound policy: simplicity, neutrality, transparency, and stability.

Urban Institute
2100 M Street NW
Washington, DC 20037
(202) 833-7200
email: media@urban.org
website: www.urban.org
The Urban Institute is a policy-focused research organization. Together with the Brookings Institution, this organization operates the Urban–Brookings Tax Policy Center. The Urban Institute collaborates with legislators, community leaders, and corporations to identify problems and design solutions.

For Further Reading

Books

Steven A. Bank, Kirk J. Stark, and Joseph J. Thorndike. *War and Taxes.* Washington, DC: Urban Institute Press, 2012. This book studies six conflicts spanning the Revolutionary War to the present-day war in Iraq to address the connection between the US tax system and its wars.

W. Elliot Brownlee. *Federal Taxation in America: A History.* Cambridge, UK: Cambridge University Press, 2016. This is a comprehensive historical overview of federal taxation in the United States.

David Callahan. *The Givers: Wealth, Power, and Philanthropy in a New Gilded Age.* New York, NY: Random House, 2017. David Callahan explores the profound social and political power wielded by the contemporary philanthropists.

Kathryn Edin and H. Luke Shafer. *$2.00 a Day: Living on Almost Nothing in America,* Wilmington, MA: Mariner Books, 2015. Academics Edin and Shafer found that 1.5 million Americans live on $2.00 a day. This book tells the stories of those families and the political and cultural system that allows for such extreme poverty.

John Galbraith. *The Affluent Society.* New York, NY: Houghton Mifflin, 1958. An influential treatise on wealth and inequality by one of President Kennedy's financial advisers.

David Graeber. *The Utopia of Rules: On Technology, Stupidity, and the Secret Joys of Bureaucracy.* Brooklyn, NY: Melville House, 2015. Anthropologist David Graeber takes an incisive look at the history of rules, regulation, and bureaucracy.

Jacob Hacker and Paul Pierson. *American Amnesia: How the War on Government Led Us to Forget What Made America Prosper.* New York, NY: Simon & Schuster, 2015. Two political scientists argue that a strong government can yield prosperity.

Michael Hitzik. *The New Deal: A Modern History.* New York, NY: Simon and Schuster, 2011. A Pulitzer Prize–winning author provides an insightful history of President Roosevelt's New Deal.

Patricia Illingworth. *Giving Well: The Ethics of Philanthropy*. Oxford, UK: Oxford University Press, 2013. Experts on the subject of giving identify and address the most urgent moral questions arising today in the practice of philanthropy.

Jane Mayer. *Dark Money: The Hidden History of the Billionaires Behind the Rise of the Radical Right*. New York, NY, 2016. Jane Mayer, a writer for the *New Yorker,* shows how a gaggle of gazillionaires, the right-wing Koch brothers chief among them, have spent billions to shape the government to their liking.

Alvin Rabushka. *Taxation in Colonial America*. Princeton, NJ: Princeton University Press, 2015. This book examines the American colonies through their tax systems to get to the heart of the causes of the revolution.

Joseph E. Stiglitz. *The Great Divide: Unequal Societies and What We Can Do About Them*. New York, NY: W. W. Norton & Company, Inc., 2016. In this book, the Nobel Prize–winning economist focuses on inquality and how it can be addressed.

Vanessa Williamson. *Read My Lips: Why Americans Are Proud to Pay Taxes*. Princeton, NJ: Princeton University Press, 2017. A Harvard-trained expert in governance shows that most Americans view taxpaying with civic pride.

Edmund Wilson. *The Cold War and the Income Tax: A Protest*. New York, NY: Farrar, Straus and Giroux, 1963. One of the nation's greatest literary critics was also a prolific tax dodger. In *The Cold War and the Income Tax*, Edmund Wilson offers a moral, and personal, critique of the income tax.

Periodicals and Internet Sources

Marina Bolotnikova. "Tax Collection and Civil Society," *Harvard Magazine,* 2017.

John Brooks. "The Tax," *New Yorker,* 1965.

Ronald Brownstein. "How Much Do Tax Cuts Really Matter?" *Atlantic,* September 21, 2017. https://www.theatlantic.com/politics /archive/2017/09/how-much-do-tax-cuts-really-matter/540498.

Jonathan Cohn. "Moral Arguments for Soaking the Rich," *New Republic,* 2010.

Charlotte Crane. "How the 100-Year-Old Income Tax Unleashed the Modern U.S. Economy," *Atlantic,* 2013.

Alain De Botton. "Utopian Tax," *The Book of Life,* 2016.

Editorial. "Don't Mess with Taxes: A Moral Defense," *New Republic,* 2011.

Alexander Hamilton. "Federalist No. 30," *The Federalist Papers,* 1787.

Julie Hirschfeld Davis and Alan Rappeport. "Trump Proposes the Most Sweeping Tax Overhaul in Decades," *New York Times*, September 27, 2017. https://www.nytimes.com/2017/09/27/us/politics/trump -tax-cut-plan-middle-class-deficit.html.

Danielle Kurtzleben. "We Asked People What They Know About Taxes. See If You Know The Answers," NPR, 2017.

Jill Lepore. "Tax Time: Why We Pay," *New Yorker,* 2012.

Patrick McVay. "Kind of a Funny Story About Death and Tax Returns," *Boston Globe,* April 4, 2017. https://www.bostonglobe.com /magazine/2017/04/04/dad-tax-collector/mjqBOzFB32FRg 8PFz45p0L/story.html.

Ben Metcalf. "Why I Pay My Taxes," *Harper's,* 2008.

Richard Rubin. "Talking Taxes: What's Your Fair Share?" *Wall Street Journal,* June 1, 2017. https://www.wsj.com/articles/talking-taxes -whats-your-fair-share-1496309401.

Gene B. Sperling. "A Tax Proposal That Could Lift Millions Out of Poverty," *Atlantic*, October 17, 2017. https://www.theatlantic.com /business/archive/2017/10/eitc-for-all/542898.

Jeff Spross. "In Praise of the Land Value Tax," *The Week*, May 5, 2015. http://theweek.com/articles/553242/praise-land-value-tax.

Ben Steverman. "Sorry America, Your Taxes Aren't High," Bloomberg, April 11, 2017. https://www.bloomberg.com/news /articles/2017-04-11/sorry-america-your-taxes-aren-t-high.

James Stewart. "Tax Me If You Can: The Things Rich People Do to Avoid Paying Up," *New Yorker,* 2012.

Olivia Waxman. "Why Americans First Started Paying a Separate Tax on Gas," *Time*, June 6, 2017. http://time.com/4803516/gas-tax -history.

Websites

Internal Revenue Service (www.irs.gov)
The IRS is the United States' tax collection agency.

Investopedia (www.investopedia.com)
A website devoted to financial news and analysis. It is also a great resource for understanding fiscal terminology.

Tax Foundation (www.taxfoundation.org)
The Tax Foundation is a nonprofit that conducts research and works to influence tax policy.

Tax Policy Center (www.taxpolicycenter.org)
The Tax Policy Center provides economic and social analysis of tax issues.

Index

Planned Parenthood, 17
Pollock v. Farmers' Loan, 12, 24
poverty, 24, 38, 55, 68, 82, 90, 107
Powell, James Lawrence, 67
progressive taxation, 24–25, 42–46, 83, 98–104
Public Works Administration, 16, 31–32

R

Reagan, Ronald, 8, 18, 59, 76, 107
Revenue Act of 1861, 8, 22, 105
Ritz, Robert A., 77
Rockefeller Foundation, 14
Romney, Mitt, 25, 38, 88, 89
Roosevelt, Franklin D., 14, 26–34, 36–37, 38, 39, 106, 107
Roosevelt, Theodore, 13
Rosenman, Mark, 87–91
Rubin, Robert, 27
Ruml, Beardsley, 14
Ryan, Paul, 89, 106

S

Sadowsky, James, 47–52
Samuelson, Paul, 48
Samwick, Andrew, 60
Sanger, Margaret, 17
Shaefer, H. Luke, 107
sin taxes, 47–52
Sixteenth Amendment, 8, 20, 24, 36, 105

Smith, Adam, 43–46
social cost of carbon (SCC), 65–72, 73–79
sugary drinks, taxes on, 53–57
Sunstein, Cass, 76, 78

T

Taft, William, 13
taxation
arguments against, 11–18
arguments for, 19–25, 35–40
flat taxation, 98–104
history of, 8, 11–18, 19–25, 105, 106
progressive taxation, 24–25, 42–46, 83, 98–104
and prohibition of charitable giving, 89
and relation to economic growth, 8, 58–64
Tax Foundation, 61–62
Tax Policy Center, 50, 95, 108
trickle-down economics, 108
Trump, Donald, 8, 59, 66, 106
$2.00 a Day: Living on Almost Nothing in America, 107
Tyranny of the Status Quo, 50

U

UN Framework Convention on Climate Change, 70, 71

V

VAT, 83–84

W

War on Poverty, 107
Warren, Elizabeth, 9
Washington, George, 49, 105
Wealth of Nations, The, 45
Weinzierl, Matthew C., 35–40
Whiskey Tax, 49, 105
Whitehouse, Sheldon, 93, 95
Wihbey, John, 73–79
Williamson, Vanessa, 8
Wilson, Woodrow, 13
Wilson-Gorman Tariff Act, 24, 105